THE BIG BOOK OF
DRESSING UP

THE BIG BOOK OF
DRESSING UP

40 fun projects

LAURA MINTER
& TIA WILLIAMS

Contents

Dinosaurs

Space

Knights

Princesses

Superheroes

Pirates

Mermaids

Introduction

Kids are fickle little fiends. One minute they want to be a mermaid, the next it's all about dinosaurs and superheroes or some strange mash-up of all three! If you know a child who loves nothing more than crafting and dressing up then you've come to the right place. *The Big Book of Dressing Up* is the ultimate book of DIY costumes to cater for all imaginations. You can create a huge range of outfits to dress head to toe as a dinosaur, astronaut, mermaid, knight, superhero, princess, or pirate! You'll find a mixture of costumes and accessories to make for each look, plus some fun scene-setters. The pages are filled with tons of inspiring ideas that can be adapted to loads of other things too.

The 40 projects in this book are all easy to follow with step-by-step instructions and accompanying photographs to help you along the way. All the projects are suitable for beginners and lots of them can be done by children with adult supervision and assistance. Some of the projects, such as the ones that require a sewing machine, are a little more tricky but children can still get involved. Little ones can sit on your knee and help steer the fabric for example, and older children can pick out the fabrics and help with the measuring and pinning.

Letting the children take the lead on a craft project is really important – they will be so much prouder of something they've made themselves, even if the finished product is a little rough around the edges. If they want their astronaut helmet to fit their toy bunny instead of themselves then go with that. Or if the entire thing should be covered in pompoms and pipe cleaners then you just have to grin and bear it!

All of these projects were created with artistic input from our own children, who have been (mostly) willing guinea pigs for all manner of costume adjustments and testing. They have been to space, sailed the seven seas, and walked in prehistoric lands to test drive our ideas. If our kids didn't love a project, it didn't make it into this book!

Laura & Tia

Tools and materials

You certainly do not need tons of craft stuff to get creative. All the projects in this book use materials that you probably already have at home or are able to get hold of easily. Below is an overview of the materials and supplies that are really useful for the projects in this book – and for crafting with kids in general.

Sewing supplies

SEWING MACHINE – This is not essential for these projects but using one will save you time and will result in a stronger, more durable result. Sewing machines can be daunting to a beginner, but they really don't need to be. Take a little time getting to know your machine, trying out all the different stitches on scraps of fabric, and sewing pieces together. It very quickly becomes addictive!

IRON-ON ADHESIVE – This clever product enables you to fuse fabrics together without having to do any stitching. It comes in fine sheets that can be cut to size then simply ironed onto the fabric. Just bear in mind that once it's stuck, it's stuck!

FABRICS – Having a good stash of fabric is always handy. Felt and fleece are our favorite fabrics for kids and beginners as they don't fray. Don't throw away scraps as they are really useful for adding details.

EMBELLISHMENTS AND TRIMS – These are great for kids' sewing projects as they are so versatile.

OTHER – Sewing threads, pins, needles, tailor's chalk, seam rippers (for when you go wrong!), and fabric scissors are all really useful.

Craft supplies

GLUE – PVA glue is fantastic for children; it's inexpensive and can be mixed with water to create papier-mâché paste, or mixed with acrylic to create a paint that adheres really well to plastics. For parents, glue guns are invaluable because the glue dries incredibly quickly and holds very well. As the glue gets hot, the guns are best handled by adults, but they make a great back-up for when your child's own sticking won't cut the mustard!

TAPE – We swear by double-sided tape for mess-free crafting with kids. It instantly sticks together card, paper, and felt, and you can buy strong-sticking varieties too, making it a more child-friendly alternative to superglue. Duct tape is great for adding color to projects and it's also really tough and durable. Masking tape is handy for creating a relief effect (where you paint over the tape and your surface then remove it) and for holding projects together while the glue dries.

CLAY AND DOUGH – Soft polymer clays, such as Fimo and Sculpey, are great for children and perfect for small items like jewelry, while air-dry clay is cheaper, really easy to use and can be painted once dry. Salt dough is also fab for kids. You can make it really easily with store-cupboard essentials, then bake it, paint it and varnish it for an indestructible finish.

PAPER AND CRAFT FOAM – Having a little stash of beautiful, sparkly paper and card is great for kids to create things on their own. Craft foam is a fantastic material for children as it is more durable than card and you can easily draw on it and cut it with scissors.

PAINT – Acrylics are best for adding strong, permanent color. If children are using them they must be supervised, with clothes and surfaces protected. You can use kiddie paints instead if you like but bear in mind the end result probably won't last as well.

PERMANENT COLORED MARKERS – Permanent pens, like Sharpies, are great for adding stay-on color without having to dig out the paints. Obviously you need to take care as kids will treat these pens like felt tips and if you turn your back you may find your child has tattooed the baby or created their own wall art!

SHRINK PLASTIC – This is wonderful for kids to play with. Everyone loves seeing their creations curl up and shrink to a tenth of their size. The finished result is strong and durable. Make sure you use permanent pens or wax coloring pencils to add the color or it will smudge onto your fingers once shrunk.

Other essentials

For crafting in general, having a good stash of these materials is always handy:
- Kids' paintbrushes in a variety of sizes
- Old mixing bowls, spoons and cups for mixing up paint, papier-mâché and Plaster of Paris
- Child-friendly scissors
- Old newspapers
- Pipe cleaners and pompoms

Craft rummage box

Keep a box full of interesting things you would otherwise recycle or throw out. Kids enjoy diving into a box, seeing what they can pull out and then magicking it into something super. Shoe boxes, cardboard tubes, egg cartons and scraps of fabric have all been transformed in this book with the help of a little paint and a glue stick (and maybe a parent in the background with a glue gun!).

It is also a good idea to keep a box with small compartments (a toolbox is ideal) for little things like pompoms, sequins, glitter and so on. This way kids can pick and choose from their very own treasure chest of wonderful crafty goodies.

Dinosaur head mask

Made from a shoebox, this fabulous T. rex head mask is perfect for stomping around the house in. It has an open mouth that acts as a visor to see out of. If you can't find upholstery foam to pad the inner mask, you could try cutting up dish sponges instead.

You will need

Shoebox big enough to fit on your head
Pen and scissors
Scrap paper or newspaper
Masking tape
Newspaper
PVA glue
Green paint and paintbrush
1 sheet of white craft foam, about
    8 x 12in (20 x 30cm)
Scraps of black and green craft foam
30in (75cm) strip of 1in (2.5cm)-thick
    upholstery foam

Step 1

To form a rounded nose shape, turn the base of the shoebox upside down and draw curved edges onto one of the narrow ends. Open up that side of the box and cut slits up to the curve. Fold along the pen lines you drew and tape the box back together so that it has rounded corners.

Step 2

Scrunch up a ball of paper the same width as the box. Tape it to the bottom at the opposite end of the rounded nose, to create a head shape.

Step 3

Add more masking tape to smooth the paper into a more even shape.

Step 4

Scrunch two more pieces of paper to the size of a golf ball and tape to the rounded end to resemble nostrils. Add more tape to smooth as before.

Step 5

To make the dinosaur's jaw, cut most of the top off the lid so you are able to fit your head through the hole.

Step 6

Tape the lid onto the bottom of the box at an angle, to look like the mouth is open. Check the fit – you should be able to see out through the "mouth". Once you are happy with the angle, cover the whole box with papier-mâché. Mix two parts glue to one part water and use small bits of newspaper to cover the head. Leave to dry overnight, then add a second layer.

Step 7

Paint the head green, using several coats of paint.

Step 8

Add facial features. For the eyes, cut two ovals from white craft foam, measuring about 2½in (6cm). Cut another oval slightly bigger from green craft foam and cut this in half to create eyelids. Cut two small circles (about 1in/2.5cm) for the pupils and two arches (about 1½in/4cm) for the nostrils, from black craft foam. Glue onto the face as shown.

Step 9

Make the teeth by cutting zigzags along the length of a piece of white craft foam.

Step 10

Glue the teeth around the inside of the mouth on the top and bottom.

Step 11

Finally, push the piece of upholstery foam inside the box. Check the fit on the child and adjust the foam so that it is in the right position to hold the mask in place and add a little padding. When you are happy with the fit, glue the foam in place and trim the ends.

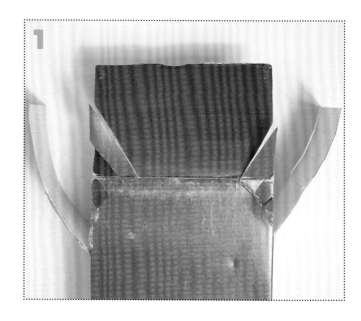

2

3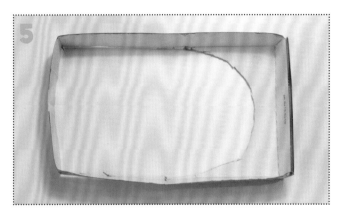

4

5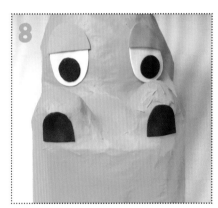

6

7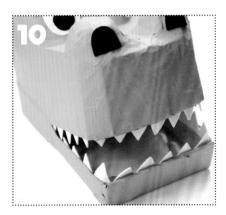

8

9

10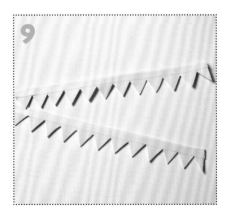

11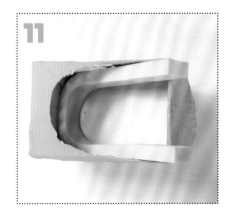

Dinosaur paws

Become a stomping T. rex with these dinosaur paws. Spray paint is best for this project as it gives great coverage, but you could use normal paint if you prefer. Bear in mind the foam tends to absorb the paint and the result may be a little patchy. Wear your paws with the cape on page 22 for a total prehistoric transformation!

You will need

30 x 20in (75 x 50cm) of upholstery foam, 2in (5cm) thick
14 x 10in (35 x 25cm) of upholstery foam, 1in (2.5cm) thick
Pen or pencil
Sharp knife or craft knife
Sewing pins
Embroidery thread
Plastic sewing needle
Sheets of newspaper
Green spray paint
Scraps of black craft foam
Black duct tape
Strong glue

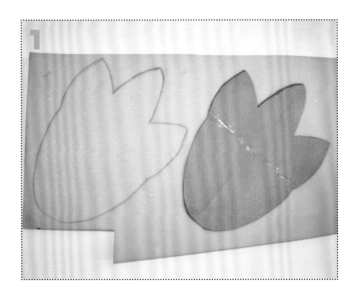

Step 1

Use the templates on page 170 for the Dinosaur Paws. Draw the shape of two paws onto the thicker foam. Use the template of the foot cover to draw two of them onto the thinner foam.

Step 2

Use a sharp knife or craft knife to cut out each paw and foot cover. An adult should do this.

Step 3

Take one of the foot covers and place in the center of the paw, with the rounded edge just under the toes. Squeeze the sides together so the foam forms a slight arch. Push pins into the foam to hold in place. Repeat for the other paw.

Step 4

Starting at one corner of each foot cover, use embroidery thread and a large plastic needle to sew the foam together (approximately ½in/1cm from the edge of the cover). Push the needle through to the base of the paw and pull taut for each stitch.

Step 5

Repeat all the way round to the other corner, leaving the flat edge open. Secure with a knot on the underside of the paw.

Step 6

Lay out some newspaper on the ground outside (or in a well-ventilated area) and ask an adult to spray the top and sides of the paws with green paint. Leave to dry.

Step 7

Cover one side of the black craft foam with black duct tape. Use the template on page 170 to draw six claws onto the back of the foam. Turn the template over so that two of the claws are facing the other direction.

Step 8

Glue the claws onto the ends of the toes.

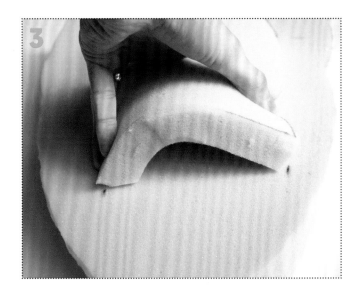

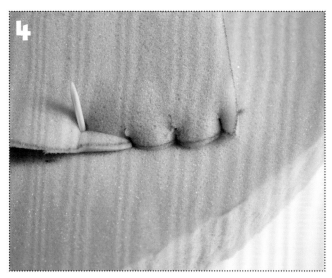

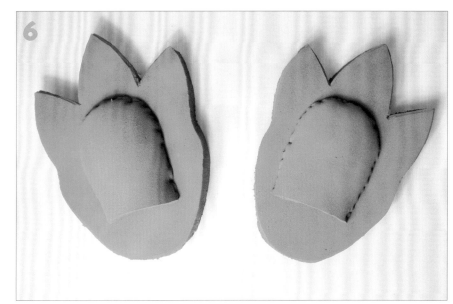

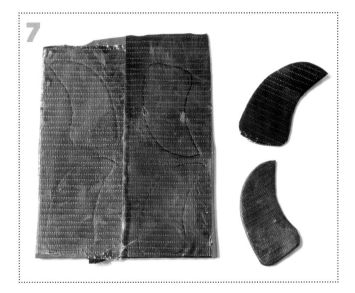

Pterodactyl wings

These fabric pterodactyl wings, which are attached to the wrists with elastic, are great fun to flap around in and they're really easy to make. If you don't have a sewing machine, you could glue the fabric scales in place using fabric glue.

You will need

Tape measure
1yd (1m) of orange cotton fabric
Scissors
Iron and ironing board
2yd (2m) of light-weight fusible interfacing
½yd (0.5m) each of yellow, orange, and brown cotton fabrics
Sewing pins
Sewing machine and matching thread (or fabric glue)
1yd (1m) of 1in (2.5cm)-wide orange bias tape
Sewing needle and thread
1yd (1m) of ½in (1cm)-wide yellow elastic

Step 1

Ask an adult to help measure you. Measure the distance between your neck and the top of your legs. Then measure from your neck to your wrist. Fold the large piece of orange fabric in half and use the measurements together with the cape diagram on page 170 to cut the piece of orange fabric.

Step 2

Following the manufacturer's instructions, iron the interfacing onto the back of the smaller pieces of yellow, orange, and brown fabrics.

Step 3

Use the template on page 170 to cut out scales from the interfaced fabrics.

Step 4

Cut out approximately 100 of these scales from the interfaced fabric.

Step 5

Starting at the bottom of the orange fabric, pin the scales on in a random color order. The scales should hang down from the bottom and cover the fabric underneath. Add another row on top, overlapping the first row. Keep going until all the orange fabric is covered.

Step 6

Using the sewing machine, sew along the straight edge of each scale with a ¼in (5mm) seam allowance. You will need to lift the overlapping scales out of the way as you go.

Step 7

Fold the orange bias tape over the top of the wings. Pin and sew in place. Cut away the excess bias tape.

Step 8

Cut two pieces of elastic measuring 8in (20cm) and two measuring 12in (30cm). Fold the shorter pieces in half and pin 2in (5cm) from each end of the wings for wrist straps. Hand stitch the wrist straps in place.

Step 9

Mark 4in (10cm) either side of the middle of the wings. Lay the two longer pieces of elastic out at these points, fold each end in by ¼in (5mm) and hand sew in place to create shoulder straps.

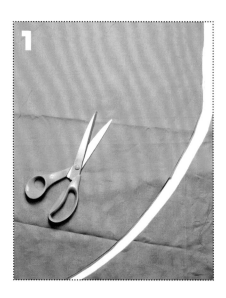

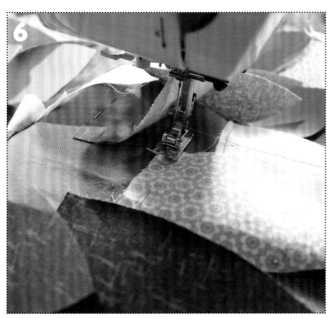

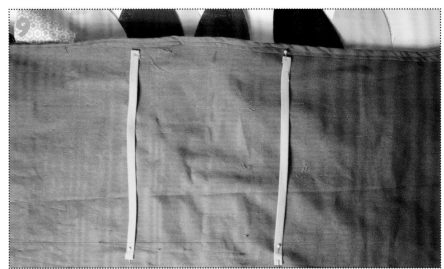

Spiny dino cape

This dinosaur cape is quicker to make than saying "Micropachycephalosaurus"!
It is made from fleece, so feels nice and furry and goes with the paws on page 14.
You will need a sewing machine for this project.

You will need

Tape measure
5½ x 5½ft (165 x 165cm) of
    green fleece
Tailor's chalk
Scissors
3 sheets of brown felt,
    about 8 x 12in (20 x 30cm)
Sewing pins
Sewing machine and
    matching thread
Sewing needle and thread
1yd (1m) of ½in (1cm)-wide
    green ribbon
1 sheet of black felt,
    about 8 x 12in (20 x 30cm)
1 sheet of white felt,
    about 8 x 12in (20 x 30cm)

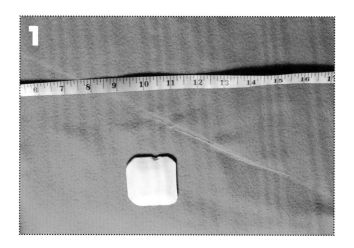

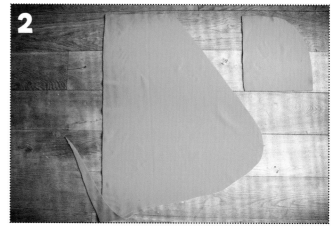

Step 1

Fold the fleece fabric in half. Use tailor's chalk to mark out the shapes of the hood and body, using the templates on page 170 as a guide for the measurements.

Step 2

Cut out two body pieces and two hood pieces from the fleece.

Step 3

Use the template on page 170 to cut out the spines from the brown felt. You will need around 15–20 spines to fill up the hood and body.

Step 4

Pin the spines facing inward along the curved edge of one of the hood pieces and the straight edge of one of the body pieces. Make sure the edges of the fabric all line up. Sew ¼in (5mm) from the edge to keep in place.

Step 5

Place the other body piece on top and pin the fabric together along the edge with spines. Sew with a ½in (1cm) seam allowance. Repeat for the hood piece.

Step 6

Open up the hood and cape. With the central seams lined up, pin the bottom of the hood to the top of the cape, right sides together, and sew with a ½in (1cm) seam allowance.

Step 7

Cut the ribbon in half and fold over each end twice by ½in (1cm) to conceal the raw edges. Pin onto each edge of the cape just under the join of the hood and body. Hand sew in place using matching thread.

Step 8

Use the template on page 170 to cut out two sets of eye pieces from the black and white felt. Sew the black part of the eye onto the white part around the edge of the black. Pin onto the hood of the cape approximately 3½in (9cm) from the front of the hood and 1½in (4cm) down from the spines. Sew in place and repeat for the other eye.

Step 9

Use the template on page 170 to cut out two sets of teeth from white felt. Pin on the inside of the hood, starting at the central seam and working outward. Trim the teeth to your preferred length and sew in place with a ¼in (5mm) seam allowance.

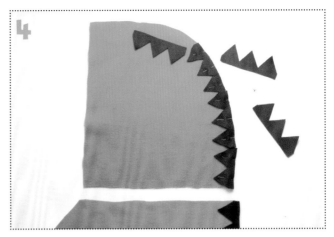

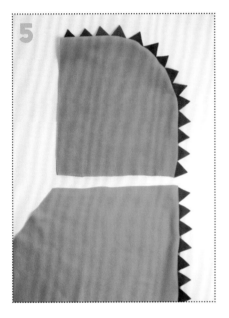

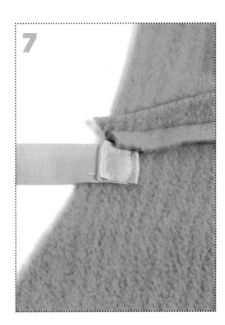

Astronaut's helmet

No astronaut's outfit is complete without a helmet, and this one is really easy and fun to make, using a balloon and a little papier-mâché – kids will love getting their hands sticky covering the helmet in gooey newspaper. Note that you will need to apply a few layers of papier-mâché to make the helmet strong – each layer must be dry before the next layer is added, so you will need plenty of patience!

You will need

Balloon
Card measuring roughly 6 x 34in
    (15 x 86cm); you can join together
    the sides of a cereal box to make
    one long strip
Masking tape
Newspaper
PVA glue and water
Pen or pencil
Scissors
White paint
White duct tape
1 x sheet of acetate about 7 x 5in (18 x 13cm)
Strong glue
Scraps of silver and blue craft foam
2 x buttons

Step 4

Paint the outside and inside of the helmet white. To give the helmet neater edges, cut small strips of white duct tape and attach them around the bottom of the helmet. Make snips into the tape to form tabs and fold the tabs under the rim. Do the same thing around the visor, but cut the duct tape in half (lengthways) first to make it thinner.

Step 5

Glue the acetate inside the helmet so that it covers the face hole.

Step 6

Photocopy the planet and planet ring templates on page 171 and cut them out. Use them to cut out a planet from the silver foam and a ring from the blue foam. Use strong glue to attach them onto the side of the helmet. Glue two buttons to the other side of the helmet, near the bottom.

Step 1

Blow up your balloon to an approximate diameter of 10in (25cm). Wrap the piece of card snugly around it, and tape the two ends of the card together with masking tape.

Step 2

The card and the top of the balloon can now be covered with papier-mâché. Tear sheets of newspaper into small pieces. Mix up the papier-mâché paste using two parts PVA glue to one part water. Working in sections, use the paintbrush to spread a layer of glue onto the card and balloon, attach the newspaper pieces, then cover with another layer of glue. Once the whole thing is covered, leave to dry overnight. Repeat the process two or three times – more layers will create a stronger helmet. When the final layer is dry, pop the balloon and remove it from the helmet.

Step 3

To create the visor, draw a 6 x 4in (15 x 10cm) rectangle about 2½in (6cm) from the bottom of the helmet, and cut it out.

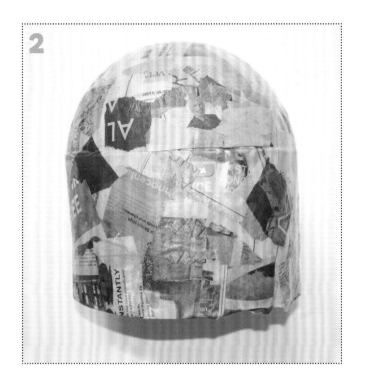

2

3

4

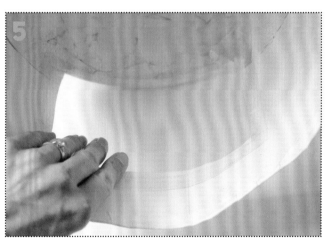

5

6

Space boots

These boots are made for (moon) walking! They're really simple to put together, too. All you need is an old pair of wellies, duct tape, and some upholstery foam, which you can pick up from a fabric or upholstery store.

You will need

Old pair of wellington boots
Approximately 36 x 12in (90 x 30cm) of
    ½in (1cm)-thick upholstery foam
White and black duct tape
Scissors
Scraps of silver and blue craft foam
Strong glue

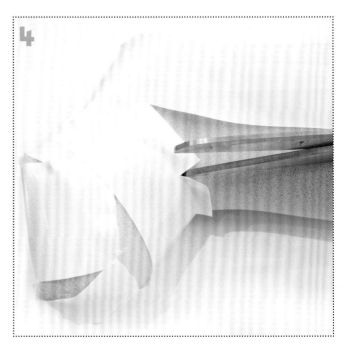

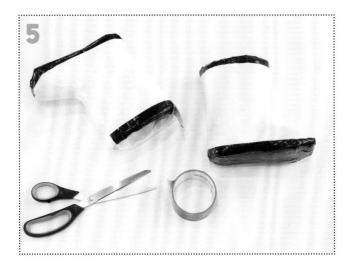

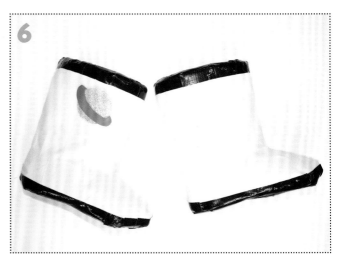

Step 1

First, you need to cover the boots with the upholstery foam, to create a padded effect. Start with the leg of the boot. Wrap the foam around it, cut to size, and tape in place using the white duct tape. Wrap another piece of foam around the toe, cut to size, and secure with tape under the sole of the boot.

Step 2

Wrap a final narrow piece of upholstery foam around the heel of the boot, and trim so that it fills the gaps (it's quite squishy so don't worry about being exact). Tape in place.

Step 3

Cover the boot all over with white duct tape. Starting with the leg, work down the length of the boot, wrapping the top of the tape over the rim and under the sole.

Step 4

Next, cover the toe of the boot. This is a bit trickier, because of the bends and curves, but you can avoid creases by snipping into the duct tape to form tabs. When the toe is covered, run tape down the front of the boot to finish.

Step 5

Cover the sole with black duct tape, making sure that the tape extends 1in (2.5cm) up the sides of the boot. Wrap short strips of black duct tape around the rim of the boot too, so that the top of the boot has a 1in (2.5cm)-thick black border. Repeat steps 1 to 5 for the second boot.

Step 6

Photocopy the planet and planet ring templates on page 171 and cut them out. Use them to cut out a planet from the silver foam and a ring from the blue foam. Use strong glue to attach them onto the outer side of one of the boots.

Walkie-talkies

Ground Control calling! These walkie-talkies are a great way for mini astronauts to keep in contact while in space. You can make them from any small cardboard boxes, but cereal selection boxes work well. The dials and knobs on the walkie-talkies can be created using lids and other scraps from the recycling bin. The instructions here are for two walkie-talkies, but you can make as many as you need.

You will need

3 x small rectangular cardboard boxes,
   e.g. small cereal selection boxes
Scissors
Masking tape
Black, white, and silver duct tape
2 x jam-jar lids
Black permanent pen
Strong glue
2 x scraps of card, each measuring
   2½ x 1½in (6 x 4cm)
Plastic drinking straw
2 x small bottle lids
4 x small buttons

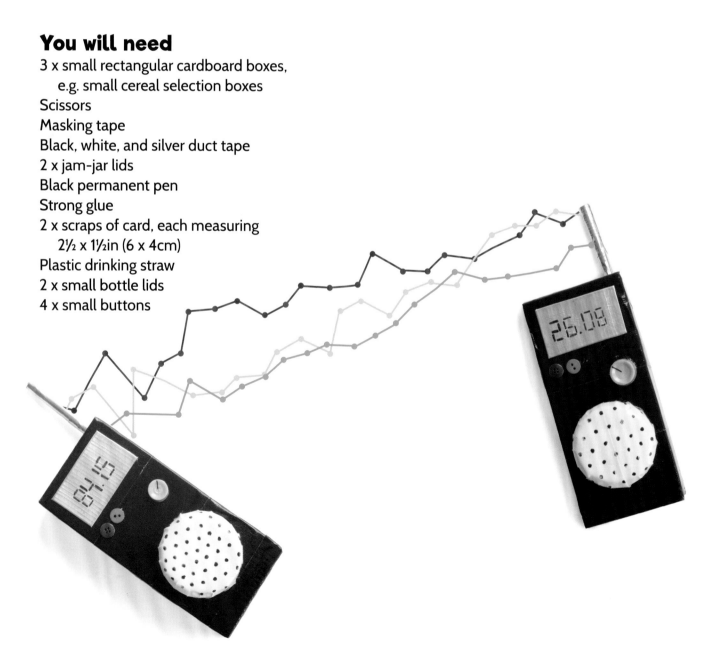

1

2

3

4

5

6

Step 1
Cut one of the cardboard boxes in half widthways. Take one of the halves and, using masking tape, attach it to the end of a second, uncut box to make a longer box. Repeat for the other box.

Step 2
Cover the ends of the boxes with black duct tape. Snip the corners and fold the excess tape neatly down the sides. Then wrap strips of black duct tape widthways around the boxes so that they are completely covered.

Step 3
To create the speakers, take the two jam-jar lids and cover them with white duct tape. Cut tabs in the excess tape and fold over the edges.

Step 4
Using a black permanent pen, draw black dots on the front of the jam-jar lids. Use strong glue to attach the lids onto the walkie-talkies, near the bottom.

Step 5
To create the walkie-talkie screen, wrap a 2½ x 1½in (6 x 4cm) rectangle of card in silver duct tape. Add digital numbers using a black permanent pen, and glue to the top of the walkie-talkie.

Step 6
To make the aerials, cut a drinking straw into 2½in (6cm) pieces and cover with silver duct tape. Glue onto the top of each walkie-talkie, in the corner.

Step 7
Take the two small bottle lids, and draw a line on each of them so that they resemble a dial. Use strong glue to stick the dials onto the walkie-talkies. Attach two small buttons to each walkie-talkie underneath the screen.

Rocket pack

This rocket pack is the coolest space accessory an astronaut can own. It's easily made from plastic bottles, and comes with flaming boosters and a fuel gauge to make sure you don't run out of gas while flying through the galaxy. The nylon straps are available to buy in craft stores and online, but they're not essential – if you can't find them, just use wide cotton tape or ribbon.

You will need

2 x 3½-pint (2-liter) plastic bottles, empty and
    with labels and lids removed
Newspaper
PVA glue and water
Paintbrush
Strong glue
Red and white paint
2 x paper cups
Scissors
70in (180cm)-long nylon strap
    and 2 x sets of buckles

1 x sheet each of red, orange, and blue felt,
    measuring 12 x 8in (30 x 20cm)
Plastic drinking straw
Masking tape
Black permanent pen
Scraps of blue and silver craft foam

Step 1
Tear the newspaper into small pieces. Make a papier-mâché paste by mixing two parts PVA glue to one part water. Working in sections, use the paintbrush to spread a layer of glue onto the bottle, attach the newspaper pieces, then cover with another layer of glue. Cover both bottles completely with newspaper and leave to dry.

Step 2
Once dry, line up the two bottles lengthways, and use strong glue to stick them together. Once the glue is dry, paint both bottles red.

Step 3
To create the boosters, cut out the base of the paper cups and paint the cups red, inside and out. Once they are dry, glue them onto the lid end of each bottle.

Step 4
Cut the length of nylon strap in half to create two pieces, each measuring 35in (90cm). Thread a buckle onto each end of both straps, then fold over the ends of the straps by 1½in (4cm) and glue to secure in place.

Step 5
Use strong glue to attach the straps along the length of each bottle, with the buckles lined up in the center.

Step 6
To make the flames, cut two strips of 4in (10cm)-wide red felt to fit inside the rim of the paper cups, then cut into the strips to create flame shapes. Repeat with the yellow and blue felt, but cut each pair slightly narrower to get a layered effect.

Step 7
For each set of flames, glue the three layers of felt together, then attach them to the inside rims of the paper cups, using strong glue.

Step 8
To make the fuel indicator, cut a 3in (8cm) piece of plastic drinking straw. Wrap masking tape around the middle of the straw and paint the other half white. Once dry, remove the tape and use a permanent pen to add lines all along the straw. Cut out a rectangle of blue craft foam slightly larger than the straw, and glue the straw in the center. Then attach the fuel indicator to the rocket pack using strong glue.

Step 9
Photocopy the planet and planet ring templates on page 171 and cut them out. Use them to cut out a planet from the blue foam and a ring from the silver foam. Use strong glue to attach them to the rocket pack top.

3
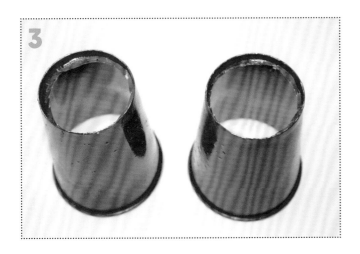

4
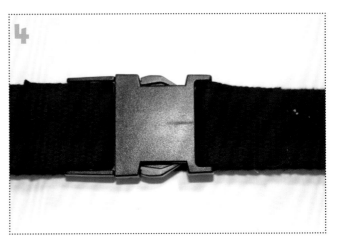

5
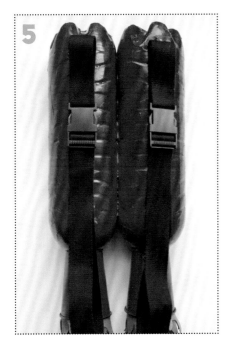

6
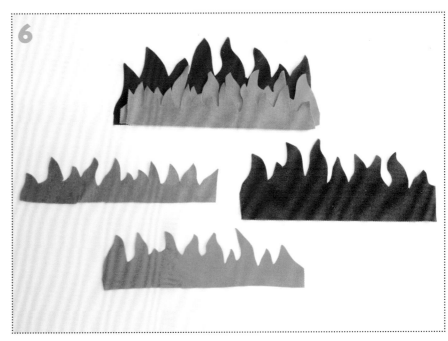

7
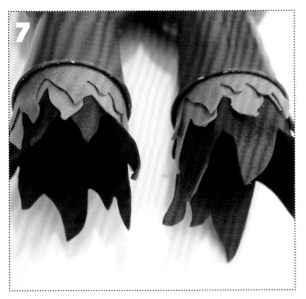

8
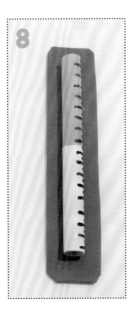

9

Giant rocket den

5... 4... 3... 2... 1... Blast off! What child wouldn't love hiding away in a giant rocket den? To create this fab space shuttle you will need a few large cardboard boxes, some bottle lids, and a bit of duct tape to hold it all together. The supplies listed below are just guidelines – have a rummage through your recycling box and see what you can find that looks as if it might belong on a rocket. You can use whatever size boxes you can find – the bigger the better!

You will need

3 x large (about 27½in/70cm) square
    cardboard boxes
Silver duct tape
Sharp serrated knife
Blue paint
Paintbrush
Silver spray paint

Selection of jar and bottle lids, including a large
    lid (such as a laundry detergent bottle)
Glue gun
A4 sheets of silver, blue, and red craft foam
Black felt-tip pen
Small and large dinner plates
Scissors

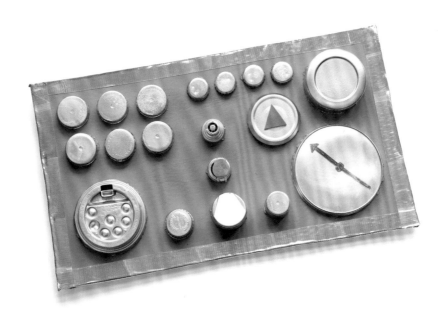

Step 1

Begin by cutting off the top flaps from two of the boxes. Take two of the removed flaps and cut in half diagonally to create four rocket feet.

Step 2

Take the third box and cut apart along the folds, removing the flaps, to create four main square panels. To turn these panels into the top pyramid of the rocket, measure halfway along one edge to find the center point on each panel. Then draw a diagonal line from that point to the bottom corners to create a triangle. Cut each one out.

Step 3

Paint the pyramid triangles and feet triangles blue. Paint the feet on both sides. Leave to dry.

Step 4

Open the bottom flaps of one of the boxes and insert the box, flaps down, into the top of the other box so that you have one tall open box. They should fit neatly together without having to tape together, but tape using duct tape if necessary.

Step 5

Make the rocket door by drawing a large rectangle (you can draw around one of the removed flaps for this) in the center of the bottom box. Add rounded edges and cut out using a sharp serrated knife, leaving a hinge on one of the long sides. Be sure to cut through the flap (from the top box) on the inside, too.

Step 6

Draw around a large detergent bottle lid about halfway down the door for the handle. Cut out the circle using a sharp serrated knife. Paint the door blue on both sides. Spray paint the detergent lid silver and leave to dry.

Step 7

Use a small dinner plate to cut circular windows in three sides of the rocket (leaving the back wall for the control panel) in the top box. Cut out.

Step 8

Use silver duct tape to tape each top triangle onto the open edges of the box. Then tape each one together to form a pyramid at the top of the rocket.

Step 9

Tape the long straight side of the rocket feet onto the bottom corners of the box using a strip of duct tape on the front and back.

Step 10

For the window frames, draw around a bigger dinner plate onto some excess cardboard. Place the original plate in the middle of the cardboard circle and draw around it to form an inner circle. Cut this out then repeat to make two more rings for each window. Spray paint them silver and glue onto the windows.

Step 11

For the control panel, cut a rectangle from one of the discarded flaps measuring about 18 x 10in (45 x 25cm). Paint blue and leave to dry. Spray paint a variety of different lids silver. Add a trim of silver tape around the edge of the blue card then use a glue gun to stick the lids on. Glue the control panel into the rocket. You can also paint and attach any other interesting old trays, tubes, and containers for added effect.

Step 12

For the Saturn planet symbol, cut a circle from blue foam about 5in (13cm) in diameter. Make a ring to go around it from silver foam, using the width of the blue circle as a guide, then cut out. Glue them together onto the top box of the rocket.

Step 13

To make the door's pin pad, cut 10 pieces about 1in (2.5cm) square from some blue foam. Cut one larger piece about 2 x 1in (5 x 2.5cm). Trim the corners slightly then glue the buttons onto a piece of red foam in a grid pattern. Use a black felt-tip pen to add numbers to the buttons, then glue the pin pad next to the door. Glue the detergent lid into the hole on the door to act as a handle.

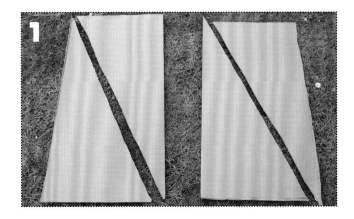

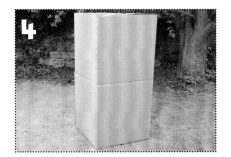

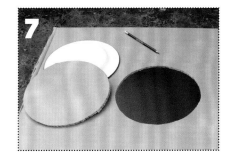

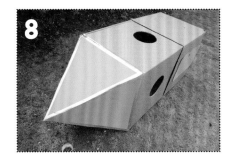

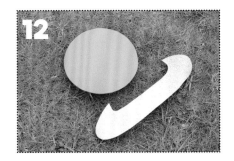

Medieval helmet

You can't be ready for battle without a helmet, and this cardboard headpiece does just the job. With a moveable visor, jaw guards, and decorative plumes on top, you can lead the charge in style and safety. This helmet is painted silver, but you could choose to cover it with foil instead for an extra shiny finish.

You will need

About 24 x 24in (60 x 60cm) corrugated card
Tape measure
Roll of masking tape
Stapler
Silver paint
Paintbrush
2 x brads (paper fasteners or split pins)
3 x colored feathers
Silver duct tape
Scissors

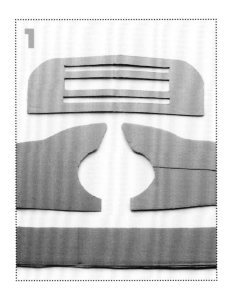

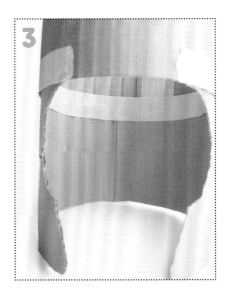

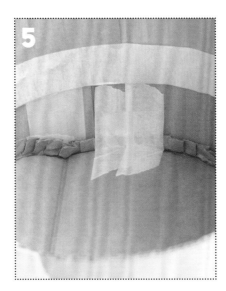

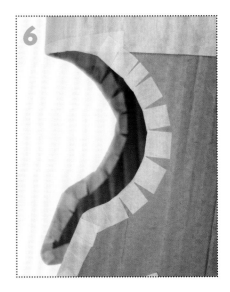

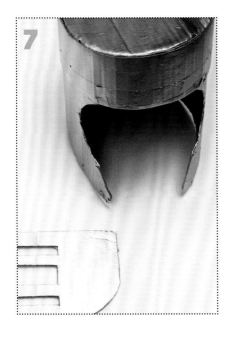

Step 1

Measure the circumference of your child's head. Cut a 2½in (6cm) wide strip of corrugated card to that length, adding an extra 3in (8cm) to the length. Photocopy the templates for the side piece and visor on page 171 and cut them out. Use them to cut out two side pieces and a visor from corrugated card.

Step 2

Use your hand to ease the card into a curved shape so it's easier to put together. Staple the head strip together with a 1in (2.5cm) overlap. Then, matching up the line on the side pieces to the bottom of the head strip, staple the side pieces in place so that there is a 3½in (9cm) gap across the front bottom corners.

Step 3

Add a strip of masking tape over all the staples so that there are no sharp edges on the helmet. Do this on the front and the inside.

Step 4

Place the helmet, top side down, onto another piece of card and draw around it from the inside (it is helpful to also mark where the back of the helmet is). Then draw another circle around it ½in (1cm) bigger. Cut out the bigger circle. Create tabs by cutting snips from the larger circle to the smaller one. Fold these tabs inward.

Step 5

Slot the circle with the tabs into the top of the helmet from the inside, and match up the back with the mark you made in step 4. Use masking tape all around the inner rim of the helmet top to keep it in place.

Step 6

Cover all the edges of the helmet with masking tape. Snip tabs into the tape where necessary to avoid creases when folded.

Step 7

Paint the helmet and visor silver, inside and out. This may need a couple of coats for an even coverage.

Step 8

To attach the visor to the helmet, mark a hole 3in (8cm) from the front of the helmet on either side. Then use brads to attach the visor to the front of the helmet, checking that it moves up and down. You might need to twist the brads a little to loosen the joins.

Step 9

For a final touch, attach three colored feathers to the back of the helmet and secure with a small strip of silver duct tape.

Royal crown

Unlike a lot of regal crowns, this one is light and comfy because it's made from foam with a fur trim. Foam is a fantastic material for craft because it's sturdier than card, it doesn't rip, and is waterproof!

You will need
16 x 24in (40 x 60cm) gold glitter foam sheet
3 x 13in (8 x 33cm) corrugated cardboard
30 x 3in (76 x 8cm) white furry fabric
14 x 14in (36 x 36cm) red velvety fabric
15 x plastic jewels, about 1in (2.5cm)
Strong glue

Adhesive tape
Stapler
1 x gold brad (paper fastener or split pin)
Craft knife
Tape measure
Scissors

Step 1

Measure the circumference of your child's head. Cut a 2in (5cm) wide strip of gold glitter foam to this length, adding an extra 2in (5cm) to the length. Cut two more strips, 1½ x 20in (4 x 50cm). Take the widest piece and staple the ends together with a 1in (2.5cm) overlap.

Step 2

Take one of the smaller strips and staple it at a right angle inside the front of the first piece. Loop it over and staple to the back. Repeat with the other strip of foam, crossing it over the first.

Step 3

Cut two strips of cardboard measuring 1½ x 13in (4 x 33cm). Curl the strips between your fingers so that they form a curve. Mark out the middle of each one then staple them together to form a downward-curving "X" shape.

Step 4

Staple the "X" shape inside the crown along the very bottom of the rim to create an internal dome.

Step 5

Place the square of red velvety fabric over the cardboard dome and arrange it so that it covers the cardboard completely. Tuck it in around the sides and then staple it in place along the rim. Trim off any excess fabric – don't worry about the bottom being neat at this stage as it will be covered later.

Step 6

Cut a 3in (8cm) wide strip of the white furry fabric to the length of the circumference of your crown. Cover it with glue and wrap it around the crown, folding 1in (2.5cm) under the rim and gluing it down on the inside.

Step 7

To make the regal shape of the crown, take a brad and push it to make a hole through the top of the red fabric in the center, and the cardboard underneath, then remove it. Push together the two foam strips on the top of the crown in the middle. Push the brad though both strips, then through the hole you previously made in the fabric and the cardboard. Secure the brad inside the crown and tape it down.

Step 8

Photocopy the crown topper template on page 171 and use it to cut two pieces from gold glitter foam. Lightly score the back along the tab line with a craft knife. Glue the pieces together with the plain sides facing, using strong glue, leaving the tabs unglued for now. Glue a plastic jewel onto the center of each side. Open up the tabs and glue the topper onto the center of the crown on top of the brad.

Step 9

As a final touch, glue plastic jewels approximately 1in (2.5cm) apart all the way around the fur trim.

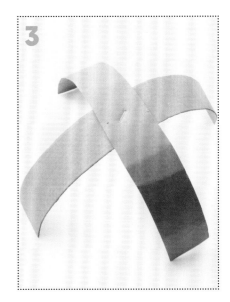

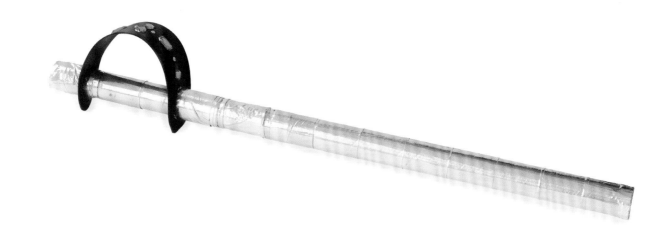

Sword and scabbard

Get ready for battle with this really simple sword, which matches the shield on page 58. It's made from recycled cardboard tubes and duct tape, so it's sturdy enough for slaying a dragon. Once a hero's work is done for the day, the sword can be stored in the handy fabric scabbard.

You will need

2 x cardboard tubes, about 12in (30cm) long and
    2in (5cm) diameter
10yd (9m) roll of silver duct tape
3 x 12in (8 x 30cm) red foam sheet
9 x plastic glue-on gems
Strong glue
40 x 6in (100 x 15cm) gray fabric
Black button, 1in (2.5cm) diameter
2 x 8in (5 x 20cm) turquoise felt
Black sewing thread
Sewing machine
Sewing needle and pins
Tape measure
Scissors
Pen

1

2

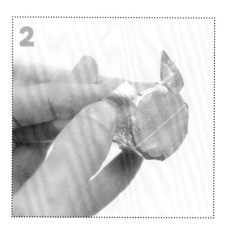

3

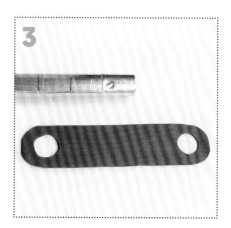

4

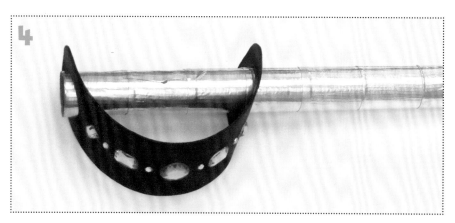

5

6

7

8

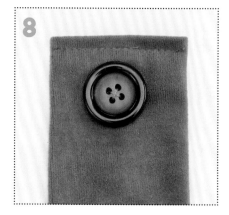

9

10

Step 1

Secure two cardboard tubes with ends together using silver duct tape. Cut strips big enough to fit around the tube and cover the whole thing.

Step 2

Cover the ends of the tube with duct tape, snipping tabs into it to enable the tape to fold over the edges without wrinkling.

Step 3

Photocopy the sword handle template on page 171 and cut it out. Use it to cut out one sword handle from red foam. If your cardboard tubes are bigger or smaller than the holes marked on the template then you will need to adjust them before cutting so that the holes fit snugly around the tube.

Step 4

Arrange and glue the plastic jewels onto one side of the foam handle, then slide it onto the tube. Add a little more duct tape onto the tube just above and below the handle to prevent it from slipping off.

Step 5

To make the scabbard, firstly measure your child's waist. The belt should hang loosely around the waist, so take this into account when taking the measurement. Add an additional 2in (5cm) for the seam allowance, then cut a piece of fabric the same length as the waist measurement and 6in (15cm) wide.

Step 6

Fold the fabric in half lengthways so that the right sides are together and pin it in place.

Step 7

Sew along the long edge with a ½in (1cm) seam allowance. Turn the fabric the right way out. Fold the ends of the fabric in by 1in (2.5cm), pin, and sew with a ¼in (6mm) seam allowance.

Step 8

Sew a button onto the fabric, 1in (2.5cm) from one end of the belt.

Step 9

On the opposite end of the belt, 1in (2.5cm) from the end, make a mark where the buttonhole will go. You can set your sewing machine to sew a buttonhole, but if you want to do it by hand, cut a slit in the fabric to the same diameter as the button. Take a needle and thread and sew around the raw edges using closely stitched blanket stitch (see below).

Step 10

Find the center of the belt and mark it with a dot of pen. Roll the piece of turquoise felt into a tube with a 1in (2.5cm) overlap and pin it onto the belt on the center point just marked. Sew it in place on the inside, along the edge of the felt. Sew another line 1in (2.5cm) along from the first line of stitching.

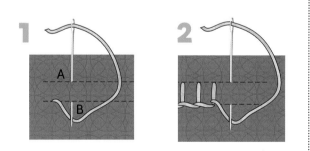

Blanket stitch looks like a row of open boxes. Pull your needle up on the baseline. Push it back down where the top of the adjoining box shape will go (A), and out at the base of that box (B). Make sure the thread is under the needle before you pull it through. Repeat.

Personalized shield

Sometimes defense is the best form of attack. This shiny shield is made using just a few household craft supplies, but can keep you safe against enemy armies. Kids can design their own crest using personalized symbols, shapes, and initials – or simply use the template provided. Combine this with the sword on page 54 and you're ready for battle.

You will need

15 x 15in (38 x 38cm) corrugated card
10yd (9m) roll of 2in (5cm)-wide silver duct tape
2 x sheets red card, 8 x 12in (20 x 30cm)
2 x sheets blue card, 8 x 12in (20 x 30cm)
2½ x 15in (6.5 x 38cm) blue craft foam
Scissors
Glue stick

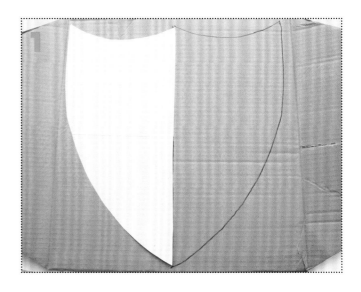

Step 1

Photocopy the template for the outer shield on page 172 and cut it out. Use the template to draw half the shield shape onto corrugated card, then flip it over to draw around the other half. Cut around the finished outer shape.

Step 2

Press a long strip of silver duct tape down the edge of one side of the shield. To prevent creases forming in the tape, cut slits on both sides of the duct tape to make tabs about 2in (5cm) apart. Then smooth the tape down on the front and back. Repeat, all around the edge of the shield.

Step 3

Cover the front and back of the shield with vertical strips of duct tape. Begin by placing a strip down the center and trim it neatly with scissors to fit each curved edge at the top and bottom. Fill up the rest of the shield, slightly overlapping each strip and trimming off any excess tape.

Step 4

Using the two inner crest templates found on page 172, draw around both pieces on red card and cut out. Flip the templates over and draw around them on blue card, then cut them out. Use the photo as a reference to arrange the crest pieces.

Step 5

You can either create your own personalized shield badges to go inside the crests, or you could use the templates provided on page 172. Cut the shield badge designs from blue card. If you are creating your own, make sure the image fits inside the space. Glue the designs onto the red crest shapes.

Step 6

For the blue parts of the crest, print or draw your child's initials onto red card and cut them out. Make sure that they fit inside the space. Glue them onto the center of the blue crest shapes.

Step 7

Glue the crest pieces onto the shield, leaving a ¾in (2cm) gap between each piece.

Step 8

To make the handle for the shield, take the strip of blue foam and stick it vertically with a piece of duct tape onto the back of the shield, 3in (8cm) down from the top.

Step 9

Loop the blue foam over downward, tuck the end under, and secure with another piece of duct tape 3in (8cm) from the bottom of the shield.

2

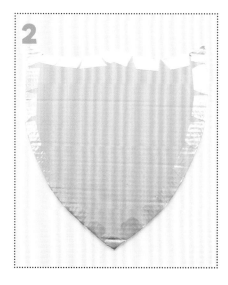

3

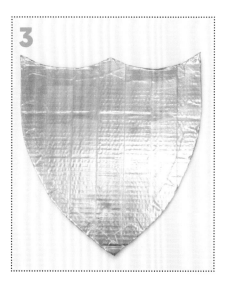

4

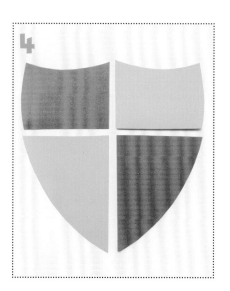

5

6

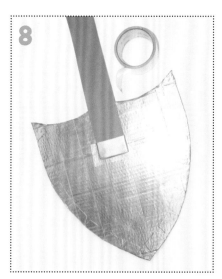

7

8

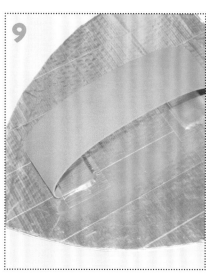

9

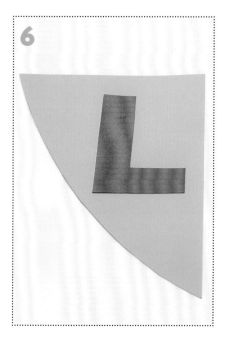

Knight's tabard

This is a really easy project to make if you're in need of a quick dressing-up costume. Your little knight can get involved too by drawing a picture for the front of their tabard. This project can be done with no sewing at all with the help of some handy iron-on bias binding and a little glue, or, if you prefer, you can use a sewing machine.

You will need

Piece of lightweight cotton fabric,
   45 x 15in (114 x 38cm)
4¼yd (4m) iron-on (or sewable) bias binding
2yd (1.8m) of 1in (2.5cm)-wide green ribbon
8 x 12in (20 x 30cm) green felt
8 x 12in (20 x 30cm) gray felt
2 x 15in (5 x 38cm) plain paper
Iron-on fabric adhesive web
A dinner plate
Tailor's chalk
Ruler
Strong glue
Scissors
Sewing needle and thread
Pins
Iron and a thin pressing cloth

Step 1

Fold the fabric in half lengthways and press. Place a dinner plate on top of the folded edge so that half of it overlaps the fabric. Use a ruler to check that the plate is lined up in the center of the fabric. Draw around the plate with tailor's chalk so that you have a semicircle and then cut it out to create a hole for the head.

Step 2

Either photocopy and cut out the dragon template on page 171 or draw your own, around 11in (28cm) high and 8in (20cm) wide. Use your template to cut one dragon shape from green felt and one from the iron-on adhesive web.

Step 3

Cut a strip of paper measuring 2 x 15in (5 x 38cm) and cut 1in (2.5cm) castellations along the top. Use this as a template to cut two decorative strips from gray felt and two from the iron-on adhesive web. To save time, you can pin the uncut template, felt and adhesive together, then cut them all out in one go.

Step 4

Lay the tabard flat and arrange the dragon motif on the center front and the gray castellated strips along the base of the tabard, front and back. The pieces of iron-on adhesive web should be sandwiched between the fabric and the felt pieces. Once you are happy with the placement of all the pieces, lay a thin pressing cloth over them and firmly iron them in place.

Step 5

Take the bias binding and carefully fold it around all the raw edges of the tabard, along each side, and inside the head hole. Pin in place and iron (or sew, if you prefer) the bias binding, to seal the edges of the fabric and prevent them from fraying.

Step 6

For the ties, cut the length of green ribbon into four pieces. Take an end of one of the pieces and fold it over ¼in (6mm). Fold over by the same amount again, and then press with an iron so that the end is nicely tucked inside. Pin the folded end onto one of the side edges on the reverse of the tabard, 10in (25cm) from the top. Sew it in place and then repeat for the other three pieces of ribbon, placing them in the same position on the other three side edges (front and back). Fold over the other end of each ribbon and stitch in place to prevent any fraying. If you want to avoid stitching altogether, simply glue the ends of the ribbons in place.

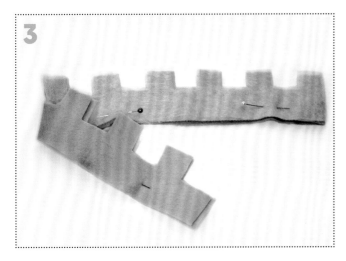

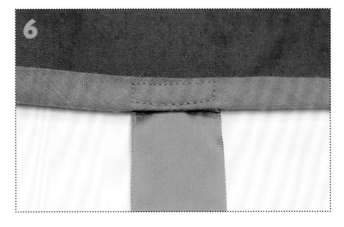

Foldaway cardboard fort

This impressive stronghold is made from large cardboard boxes and comes complete with two large rooms, a connecting tunnel, and a fully operational drawbridge. But don't feel that you have to stop at two rooms – you could continue to build up your medieval home, adding as many rooms and connections as you like.

You will need

2 x large cardboard boxes, roughly
    30 x 30 x 20in (76 x 76 x 50cm)
Large piece of corrugated cardboard,
    roughly 20 x 50in (50 x 127cm)

Craft knife
Scissors
Gray and brown paint
Paintbrush
Felt in two colors, 8 x 12in (20 x 30cm)
2 x lengths of doweling, 12in (30cm) long,
    ¼in (6mm) diameter
Strong glue
Duct tape
Pencil
Ruler
Black marker pen
20in (50cm) of ⅟₁₆in (2mm)-wide ribbon
9ft (2.75m) fake ivy or flowers (optional)

Step 1

Open the folding tops of the boxes upward and fix them together with duct tape so that they stand upright. Mark out the features of the castle onto the boxes with pen or pencil, following the diagram on page 171.

Step 2

Using a craft knife, cut out the features that you have drawn. Leave the bottom of the tunnel holes and drawbridge and one long side of the door uncut so they are still attached.

Step 3

To make the tunnel, take the long strip of corrugated card and draw a line along each of the longer sides, 2in (5cm) from the edge. Cut tabs all the way along the longer sides, from the edge of the card to the line you drew, about 2in (5cm) apart. Roll the card up to make it more pliable.

Step 4

Paint the boxes and the piece of cardboard for the tunnel gray, and the doors brown. It may take several coats to get an even coverage. Once dry, embellish the castle walls with bricks, approximately 3 x 4in (8 x 10cm), using black marker pen. Draw lines 2in (5cm) apart, vertically down the door, to create a panelled effect.

Step 5

To assemble the castle, pull down each of the tunnel openings, which are still attached along the bottom. Wrap one of the long sides of the corrugated cardboard strip inside one of the tunnel openings and stick down the tabs onto the inner castle walls using duct tape, starting from the top and working around. When you get to the bottom, tuck the excess card underneath the folded-down tunnel opening. Repeat for the other end of the tunnel so that the two boxes are connected.

Step 6

To make the drawbridge buttons, draw two circles 2½in (6cm) in diameter onto corrugated cardboard and cut them out. Mark two dots in the center of each circle, 1½in (4cm) apart. Poke through where the dots are with a pencil to make two holes. Paint the buttons gray and leave to dry.

Step 7

Make two holes with a pencil (the same distance apart as the holes you made in the buttons) 3in (8cm) down from the top of the drawbridge. Thread a 6in (15cm) length of ribbon through the holes in one of the buttons, and then through the drawbridge door. Thread the second button onto the same piece of ribbon, on the inside. Secure with a knot and cut the excess ribbon off.

Step 8

To make the loop, make a hole 1in (2.5cm) above the drawbridge on the wall of the fort. Take another 14in (35cm) length of ribbon and thread it through the hole. Wrap it around the button on the front of the drawbridge and tie it so that it is loose enough to slide on and off. Trim off any excess.

Step 9

To make the flags, cut a piece of felt measuring 3½ x 4in (9 x 10cm). Spread glue onto the felt and wrap it around the top of a length of doweling, folding in half and sandwiching together. Cut a simple motif from some scrap felt and glue on. Secure in place with duct tape.

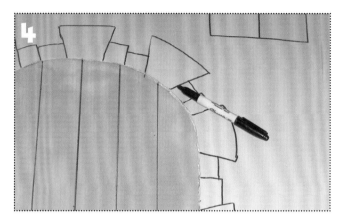

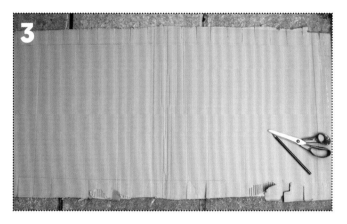

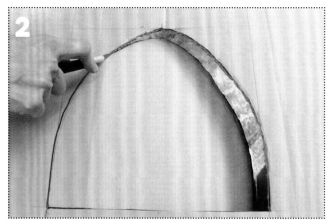

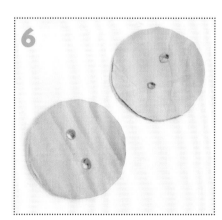

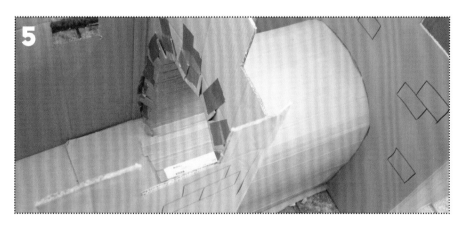

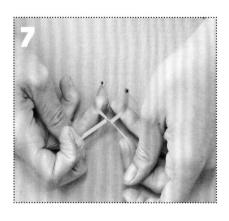

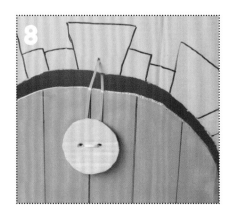

Three quick crowns

These three crowns are fantastic for all royal occasions. The mini glitter crown is attached to a hair clip, so it can be fastened onto the hair in any position, perfect for an understated royal look. The sparkly pipe-cleaner crown is so easy to make, using just two materials. Pipe cleaners are fantastic for crafting – they're cheap, versatile, and easy to work with. The felt tiara is stylish and simple. Because it stays in place with a plastic hairband, even the youngest princess can wear it without fear of it falling off. The shape can be as elaborate as you like, but remember that you will need to cut it from felt, so avoid drawing anything too fiddly.

You will need

For the mini crown hair clip:
6 x 8in (15 x 20cm) silver glitter foam
Strong glue
Hair clip
Small white pompoms
Pink acrylic paint
Paint brush
Safety pin
Scissors

For the pipe-cleaner crown:
About 14 gold or silver sparkly pipe cleaners
About 22 mixed beads, big enough to fit onto the pipe cleaners

For the felt tiara:
1 x plain plastic hair band
8 x 12in (20 x 30cm) white sparkly felt
PVA glue
Sewing needle and thread
Scissors

Mini crown hair clip

Step 1
Photocopy the crown template on page 173. Draw around it onto the glitter foam and cut it out with scissors. Roll it into a tube shape with the tab on the inside, and glue it in place. Press together and hold until the glue has set enough to stay in place.

Step 2
To make the base, place the crown on top of another sheet of glitter foam and draw around the inside. Cut this out and glue it inside the bottom of the crown.

Step 3
Glue the pompoms along the bottom outer edge of the crown and paint the inside pink. Finally, glue the hair clip onto the base and leave to dry completely – you don't want glue in your hair!

Pipe-cleaner crown

Step 1
Begin by making a hoop shape from two pipe cleaners, a little smaller than the circumference of your child's head (roughly 5in/12.5cm in diameter). Twist the ends together.

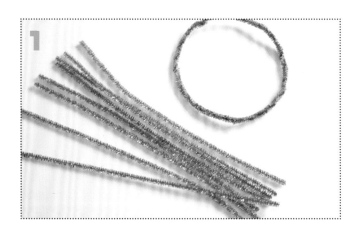

Step 2
Take another pipe cleaner and fold it in half to make an upside down "V" shape. Place a bead onto each end and slide until each one is about 3in (8cm) from the bend at the top. Twist each side of the "V" shape to secure it onto the hoop, to form the spikes of the crown.

Step 3
Repeat this process around the entire loop. Take the excess pipe cleaner ends and twist them around the hoop of the crown.

Felt tiara

Step 1

Begin by making a template for the felt. Place the hair band on a piece of paper and draw around the top curve. Draw your design for the tiara on top of this curve (fold the paper in half along the curve if you want it to be symmetrical). Add an additional ½in (1cm) below the curve to enable it to be attached to the hair band. Cut the shape out.

Step 2

Pin the template to the piece of felt and cut out two pieces – a front and a back piece (remember to turn the template over if it is not symmetrical). Glue the two pieces together, leaving the bottom ½in (1cm) tab unglued. Once dry, make snips all the way along the bottom, ½in (1cm) apart.

Step 3

Once dried, place the hair band inside these tabs. Add a little glue to the middle to stop it from sliding off the band, then fold in the tabs and hand stitch together with a needle and thread.

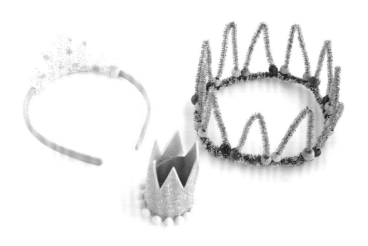

Salt-dough twinkle wand

It's magical being a princess, especially when holding your own wonderful wand. This project uses salt dough, which is very simple to make as it uses only three basic ingredients. You could make a set of wands using cookie cutters to create different shapes – decorating them would make a great princess party activity.

You will need

For the salt dough:
8oz (225g) flour
8oz (225g) salt
4fl oz (100ml) lukewarm water

For the wand:
Pink acrylic paint
Paintbrush
10in (25cm) length of doweling, ¼in (6mm) thick
Roll of pretty fabric washi tape, ½in (1cm) wide
½in (1cm) glue-on gems
Strong glue
3 x pieces of different-colored narrow ribbon, 8in (20cm) long
3 x small bells
Sewing needle and thread
Rolling pin
Star-shaped cookie cutter, about 2½in (6cm) wide
Plastic wrap

Step 1

Begin by making the salt dough. Preheat the oven to 210°F/100°C/Gas Mark ¼. Mix the flour and salt together. Add the water in small amounts, and mix together to form a dough. The dough should not be sticky or come off on your fingers. If it does, add more flour to the mix. Knead into a ball then roll out to a thickness of ½in (1cm).

Step 2

Use a cookie cutter or paper template to cut out a star shape about 2½in (6cm) wide. Poke the dowel into the bottom edge of the star to make a hole in the dough.

Step 3

Bake the star in the oven for 2–3 hours, until the dough has hardened and turned slightly brown, turning over halfway through. Remove from the oven and leave to cool.

Step 4

Once the star has cooled down, paint it all over with two coats of pink acrylic paint. Once it is dry, use strong glue to attach the gems around the edge.

Step 5

Wrap the fabric washi tape diagonally around the dowel in order to cover it completely. Secure at each end with a dab of glue.

Step 6

Check the dowel fits inside the hole in the star – it may have lost its shape a little with cooking, in which case you may need to twist the handle of a teaspoon into the hole to widen it. Put some strong glue into the hole and press the ends of each of the lengths of narrow ribbon inside. Add a little more glue, then insert the dowel, pushing it into the hole as far as it will go.

Step 7

Finally, hand stitch the small bells onto the ends of each of the ribbons.

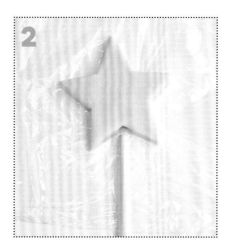

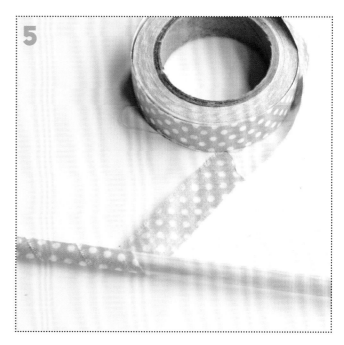

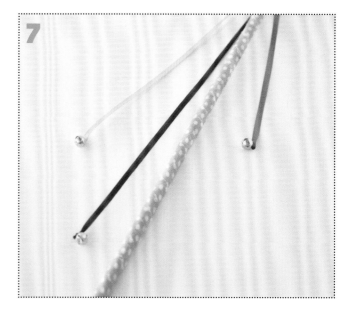

Winter princess cape

This warm and cuddly fleece cape is the perfect addition to an ice princess costume. Polar fleece is a great fabric for beginner sewers because it doesn't fray, so the edges can be left raw. The fleece could be swapped for a lighter fabric for a cooler look – the pattern is very simple and will remain the same. If you use a lighter fabric, you will need to sew the edges under or use bias binding. You can also get creative with the embellishments – this cape features pompoms and feathers, but you could try jewels, fabric paint, or even monogram the back in felt.

You will need

2yd (1.8m) of purple polar fleece
1yd (1m) of 1in (2.5cm)-wide pink ribbon
1½yd (1.25m) of pompom trim
1yd (1m) of light purple feather-boa trim
Tailor's chalk
Ruler
Safety pin
Sewing needle and matching thread
Pins
Sewing machine

Step 1

First, fold the fabric in half and mark out the shape of the cape as shown in the diagram opposite, using a ruler and tailor's chalk. Use the pattern on page 172 as a guide – the dimensions do not have to be exact because the garment is not fitted. You may find it easier to draw around a circular dinner plate to get a smooth curve for the outer cape.

Step 2

Lay the outer cape piece out flat. Then place the inner piece on top, 2in (5cm) from the top edge of the outer fabric, positioned in the center. There should be about 2in (5cm) of outer cape fabric on each side of the inner piece.

Step 3

Fold the 2in (5cm) of outer cape over the inner cape and pin together, sandwiching the fabric in place. Sew along the edge of the fabric to create a channel for the ribbon.

Step 4

Pin the length of pompom trim around the lower edge of the outer cape and sew it in place.

Step 5

Take the length of feather-boa trim and line it up around the bottom edge of the inner cape piece. Hand stitch it in place, all the way along.

Step 6

Take the ribbon and fold each end over by ½in (1cm) and secure with a few hand stitches. Attach a safety pin onto one end of the ribbon and gradually feed it through the channel at the top of the cape, wiggling and pulling it along. Hold onto one end so that it does not get lost as you pull the other end through. Tie the ribbon in a bow to hold the cape in place when being worn.

Ice princess tutu

This skirt is simply too, too elegant! Made from lightweight organza, the skirt wraps around the waist and ties with ribbon, so sizing isn't overly important. Organza is a lovely delicate fabric that comes in different weights – the finer it is, the more fiddly it will be to sew. You could also use tulle (netting) if you want a puffier, ballerina look. This project isn't as tricky as it looks, so don't be put off if you're new to sewing. Complete the look with the matching gloves on page 90.

You will need

2yd (1.8m) of pale blue organza or
    fine tulle
2yd (1.8m) of white organza or fine tulle
4¼yd (4m) of ½in (1cm)-wide blue ribbon
2yd (1.8m) of ½in (1cm)-wide white ribbon
2yd (1.8m) of 4in (10cm)-wide blue ribbon
About ten snowflake embellishments
Fabric glue
Sewing machine
Matching thread
Sewing needle
Iron
Scissors

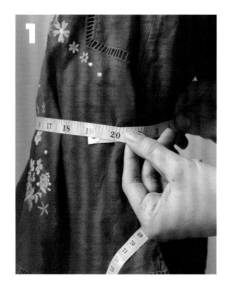

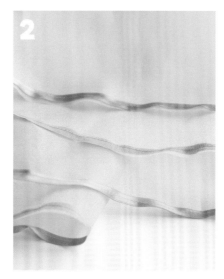

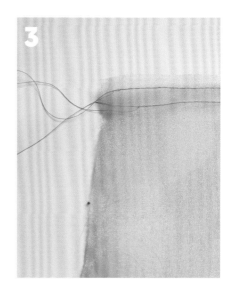

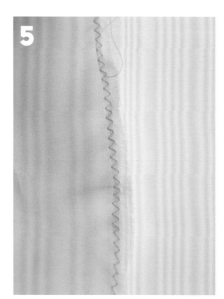

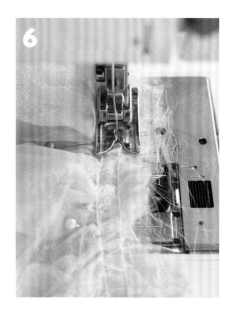

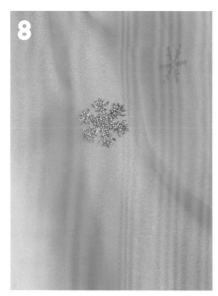

Size chart

Age (years)	Approximate waist measurement
3	20½in (52cm)
4	21in (53cm)
5	21½in (55cm)
6	22in (56cm)
7	22½in (57cm)
8	23in (58cm)
9	23½in (59cm)
10	24in (60cm)

Step 1

Begin by measuring the waist of the child who will wear the skirt. For guidance, see the sizing chart opposite. From the blue organza, cut two pieces: one 2yd (1.8m) long x 14in (38cm) wide and another piece 2yd (1.8m) long and 13in (34cm) wide. From the white organza, cut a piece 2yd (1.8m) long x 12in (30cm) wide.

Step 2

Pin coordinating ½in (1cm)-wide ribbon along the bottom edge of each piece of fabric and sew in place with matching thread.

Step 3

Set your sewing machine to the longest straight-stitch length (3 or 4). Pull the machine thread so there is 5in (12.5cm) of excess before you start to sew. Without back-stitching, sew two parallel lines of stitching along the top of each piece of fabric ½in (1cm) and 1in (2.5cm) from the top. When you get to the end, without back-stitching, cut the thread to leave a string of thread at least 5in (12.5cm) long.

Step 4

Now to ruffle and gather the fabric. From one end, take the top threads of each line in one hand. Use your other hand to pull and gather the fabric toward you. Do a little, then repeat from the other end of the fabric. Continue until the fabric has reached the same length of the waist measurement that you took in Step 1. Tie the ends of the thread together. Adjust the ruffles so that they are even, then secure in place by sewing over the gathers, on top of your original stitches (set your machine back to a normal stitch length for this).

Step 5

Sew a zigzag stitch along the short sides of each piece of fabric to stop it from fraying and neaten the edges. Trim off any excess material with sharp scissors.

Step 6

Pin the three layers of skirt together at the waistband. Use a zigzag stitch to sew them together between the previous stitch lines.

Step 7

Fold the wide piece of ribbon in half lengthways and iron it flat. Lay the ribbon out and place the waistband of the skirt in the center, sandwiched by the ribbon. Pin in place, then sew from one end of the ribbon to the other, along the open edge. Fold the ribbon ends over by ½in (1cm) and secure with a few hand stitches.

Step 8

Glue the snowflake embellishments onto the first two layers of the skirt. As you do this, be careful to keep the layers apart to prevent the glue from sticking the skirt layers together.

Rapunzel hair braid

This braid is very simple to make – all you need is a ball of yarn! This one is long and golden, just like Rapunzel's, but you could make it in a variety of colors, styles, and lengths for different princesses. Try ruby red for a mermaid or white with snowflakes for a snow queen. Involve your little one in the making process by teaching them how to do a braid.

You will need

1¾oz (50g) ball of yellow wool yarn
Scraps of pastel-colored felt
7 x colored buttons
10in (25cm) of ½in (1cm)-wide ribbon
Strong glue
Scissors
Tape measure

Step 1

Pull a strand of yarn to a length of around 47in (120cm). Fold it back on itself to create a series of loops that are the same length. Keep going until there are about 25 loops, then cut the yarn. You may want to ask someone to hold one end for you while you do this, or wrap the loops around a chair.

Step 2

Take another 47in (120cm) long strand of yarn and tie in the center of the hair to secure. The excess strands will hang to form part of the bunch. Cut through the loops at each end.

Step 3

Measure the circumference of your child's head and divide this number by two. Working from the tied center of the hair outward, make two plaits, one on each side of the center. Each of these plaits needs to measure the length of half the circumference of your child's head. Take another 1yd (1m) length of yarn and tie the two plaits together (again, the excess will form part of the bunch). You should now have a braided loop that fits on your child's head – if it is too big or too small, adjust where you tie it.

Step 4

Plait the remaining length of hair as one. Tie it at the end with another short strand of wool. Trim the ends to ensure they are all the same length.

Step 5

To make the flowers, cut small flower shapes from felt using the template found on page 172. Place one at an angle on top of another and glue them together, then glue a matching button on top.

Step 6

Glue the flowers along the hair and tie a piece of ribbon in a bow around the end of the plait.

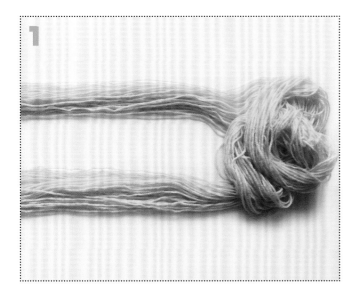

Sparkly ice queen gloves

Whether your princess is waving at crowds, or having to conceal magical powers, she'll want a pair of jeweled gloves. As the perfect finishing touch to a royal outfit, such as the tutu on page 82, these couldn't be easier to make. Shiny satin-effect gloves like the ones used here are readily available and are perfect for precious princess hands.

You will need

A pair of satin-effect dressing-up gloves
Plastic gems in a variety of sizes
13in (32cm) of silver rickrack trim
Strong glue
Gray or silver thread
A few sheets of rolled-up paper
Tweezers
Pencil
Scissors

Step 1

Begin by cutting the rickrack trim in half and pinning it around the bottom edge of the gloves.

Step 2

Hand stitch the rickrack in place using gray or silver thread.

Step 3

Place gems onto one of the gloves and play around with them until you are happy with the design, then using a pen or pencil, mark out where you placed each one with small dots.

Step 4

Place rolled-up paper inside the gloves to prevent them from sticking together. Use strong glue to carefully place the gems onto the gloves – use tweezers if this is a little fiddly.

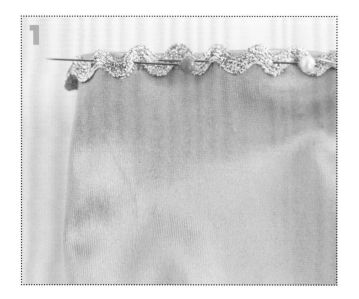

Other ideas

These gloves are super simple, but why stop there? You could add sparkle to other items too. Why not glam up a pair of ballet pumps, or a matching satin bag, for example?

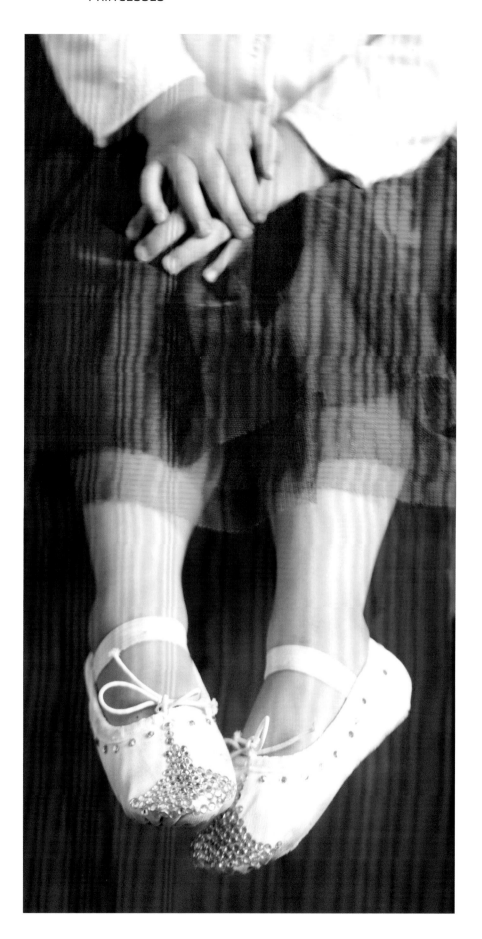

Royal horse

This beautiful steed is perfect for any royal outing. She's very well trained, as well as being easy to make, with just some simple sewing and a long piece of doweling or a broom handle being all that's needed. This regal horse has ribbon reins and a beautiful woolen mane, which could even be plaited or styled with bows and accessories.

You will need

1yd (1m) white corduroy fabric
¾oz (25g) ball of gray wool yarn
1½yd (1.25m) of ¾in (2cm)-wide
   purple ribbon
Scraps of pink felt
Black and white embroidery thread
2 x 1in (2.5cm) diameter black buttons
Broom handle or thick piece of
   doweling, at least 1in (2.5cm)
   in diameter and 1yd (1m) long
9oz (250g) bag of toy stuffing
Duct tape
Sewing machine
Sewing needle and thread
Scissors

Step 1

Photocopy the horse's head template on page 172 and cut it out. Fold the fabric in half and pin the template on top. If you are using corduroy, check the grain of the fabric before cutting so that it feels smooth when stroked from top to bottom. Cut around the template so that you have two head pieces for the horse.

Step 2

To make the horse's mane, wrap yarn around a book measuring about 10in (25cm), 20 times to make a bundle, then cut the yarn and remove. Repeat this until you have enough bundles to fit tightly all the way down the neck of the horse (approximately 10 bundles).

Step 3

Take one of the cut-out head pieces and pin the woolen bundles on the right side of the fabric, along the horse's neck. Start from roughly where the ears will go, down to 5in (12.5cm) from the bottom. The ends of the bundles should just overlap the edge of the fabric. Once all the bundles are pinned in place, carefully sew them onto the fabric with a ¼in (6mm) seam allowance.

Step 4

Tuck the mane inside so that it is out of the way, then pin the two head pieces with right sides together. Sew them together with a ½in (1cm) seam allowance, starting at the bottom of the head and continuing all the way around to the other side, leaving the bottom open. Once sewn snip notches around the curved edges then turn the right way out. Cut the loops of yarn to finish the mane.

Step 5

Lightly fill the horse with toy stuffing. Mark on each side of the head where the eyes will be and sew on buttons. Stitch the eyelashes, nostrils, and a smile by hand with black embroidery thread, using the picture on page 94 for reference.

Step 6

To make the ears, photocopy the template on page 172 and cut out four ear shapes from corduroy fabric. Cut two inner pieces from pink felt. Sew the felt onto the center of two corduroy pieces. Pin the ears with right sides together and sew with a ¼in (6mm) seam allowance, leaving the bottom open. Snip around the curved edges then turn the right way out. Press, folding the raw edges in at the bottom. Carefully sew the ears onto the top of the head by hand. Fill the head with more toy stuffing until it is sturdy.

Step 7

For the reins, wrap ribbon around the nose, cut to size, and pin in place. Hand stitch at the bottom to secure. Tuck one end of the remaining ribbon into the nose piece by the mouth, and pin. Then take this length of ribbon under the eye, fold and pin at right angles, then over the forehead and repeat along the other side back to the nose. Pin in place and cut. The remaining ribbon will be the reins. Tuck each end under the folded corners and then carefully hand stitch all the pinned sections down.

Step 8

Before inserting the doweling or broom handle into the horse, add a stopper to hold it in place and prevent it from ripping the fabric. Do this by wrapping a ball of scrap fabric around the top and securing this in place firmly with duct tape. Push the doweling into the head. Add more stuffing so that the doweling does not touch the fabric and sits solidly in the center of the head.

Step 9

Fold up the bottom hem by 1in (2.5cm) and, using white embroidery thread with a knot tied in the end, hand sew a long running stitch along the hem. Pull the thread taught to gather the fabric together, then hand sew a few stitches across the hole, and knot to secure.

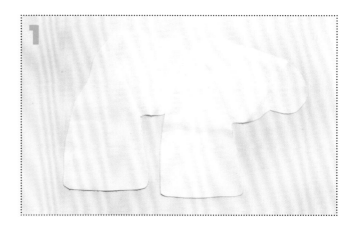

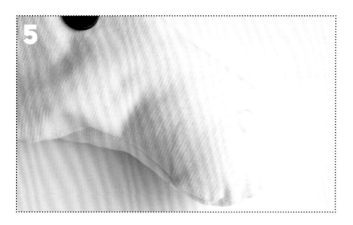

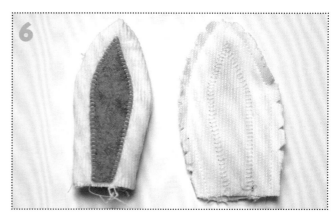

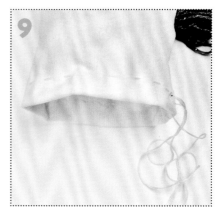

Superhero mask

Every superhero needs to conceal their true identity from the world. This reversible mask is easy to make from felt and, as well as preserving your anonymity, it will allow you to flip between two superhero characters in the blink of an eye.

You will need

9 x 4in (23 x 10cm) each of red and green felt
9 x 4in (23 x 10cm) of fusible interfacing
Scrap of yellow felt
Scissors
About 15in (38cm) of thin elastic
Yellow embroidery thread, sewing needle and pins
Iron and ironing board

Step 1

Use the template on page 173 to cut out mask shapes from red and green felt. Cut a star from red felt and fusible interfacing, and a lightning bolt from yellow felt and fusible interfacing.

Step 2

Following the manufacturer's instructions, attach the fusible interfacing onto the lightning bolt and star, using a cloth to protect the felt from melting. Remove the backing from the interfacing.

Step 3

Press the star onto the side of the green mask and the lightning bolt onto the red mask.

Step 4

Pin the two masks together with the symbols on the outside. Hand sew around the outside of the mask and inside the eye holes with yellow embroidery thread.

Step 5

Use a sharp pair of scissors to pierce a hole at the top of the mask on either side.

Step 6

Thread the elastic through the mask at both sides, fit on your superhero's head, and secure with a knot.

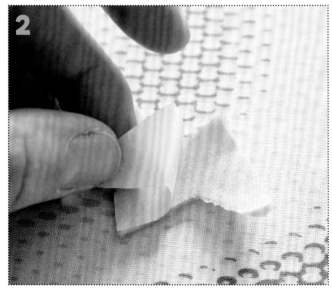

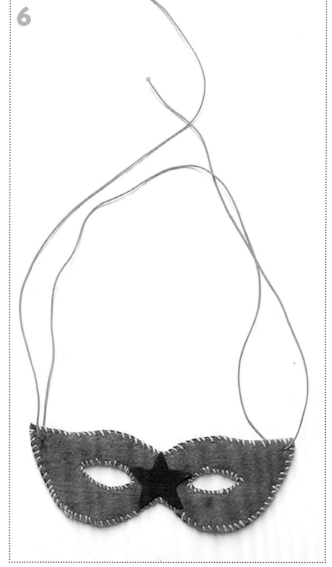

Reversible cape

This super-easy cape features star and lightning bolt emblems, but you could make it to resemble your favorite superheroes or villains, or create two new characters with personalized emblems featuring your initials. The project requires a sewing machine; you could make it without one but it will take you a while to stitch around the edges!

You will need

1yd (1m) square each of green and
　　blue cotton
4in (10cm) square each of red and
　　black cotton
8in (20cm) square of yellow cotton
Scissors
Side plate about 8in (20cm) in diameter
Sewing needle and pins
15 x 35in (38 x 90cm) of fusible webbing
Sewing machine and matching thread
1½ x ½in (4 x 1cm) of Velcro
　　(hook-and-loop tape)
Iron and ironing board

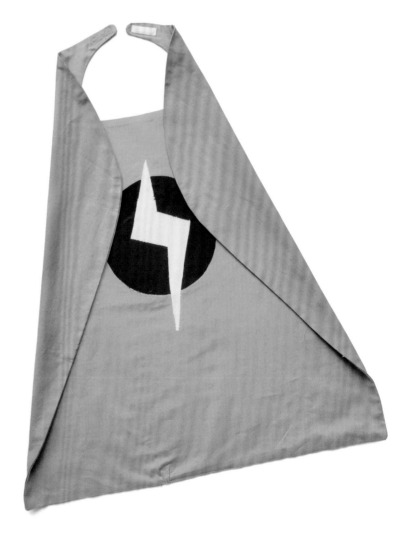

Step 1

Photocopy the cape template (see page 173) and cut it out. Fold your green fabric in half and pin the template on top. Cut out one cape shape then repeat with the blue fabric. Use a side plate to draw round and cut out a circle from yellow and black cotton. If you want to use the emblems featured here, cut out a yellow lightning bolt and a red star shape. You could draw your own or use the templates on page 173. Also cut the circles, lightning bolt, and star shapes out of fusible webbing.

Step 2

Iron the fusible webbing onto the back of each shape. Line up the yellow circle centrally on the front of the blue cape 8in (20cm) from the neckline. Iron in place, and then iron the star on top of the center of the yellow circle. Repeat with the green cape, the black circle, and the lightning bolt.

Step 3

Pin the two capes right sides together. Machine sew around the edge with a ½in (1cm) seam allowance. Leave a 6in (15cm) gap along the bottom to allow you to turn the cape right sides out. Trim the edges around the neckline of the cape then make snips in the seam allowance around the curved edges, about 1in (2.5cm) apart. This will prevent puckering.

Step 4

Turn the cape right sides out and push out all the corners and neckline. Press the cape and sew the turning gap closed by hand.

Step 5

Pin and sew one piece of the Velcro onto the end of the neckline on the blue fabric. Sew the other piece on the green fabric (at the other side) so that the two pieces line up when the neckline is joined.

1

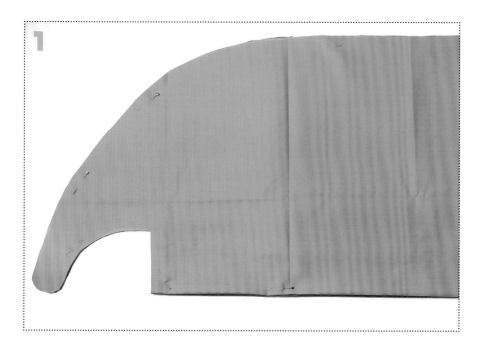

2

3

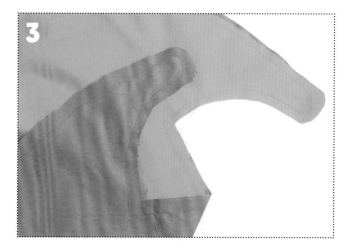

4

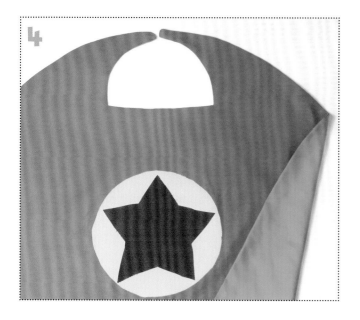

5

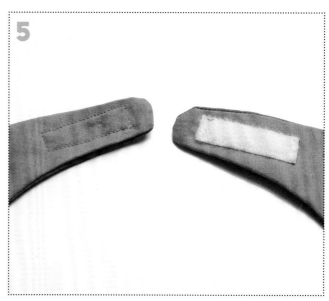

Superhero arm cuffs

Arm cuffs add the finishing touches to any superhero's outfit. These cuffs are made from fake leather, which is easy to work with as it doesn't fray, but if you prefer you could use felt. These cuffs have been made with a sewing machine, but if you don't have one or are short on time you can glue the fabric together.

You will need

10 x 8in (25 x 20cm) of gold fake leather or felt
8 x 6in (20 x 15cm) of red fake leather or felt
Scissors
Masking tape
Tracing paper or baking parchment
Sewing machine and matching thread
Fabric glue
2 x 4in (10cm) strips of Velcro
    (hook-and-loop tape)

1

2

3

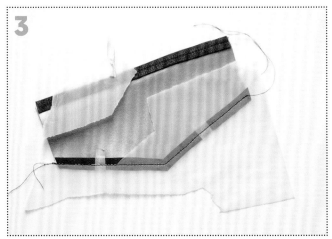

4

5

Step 1

Photocopy the template on page 173 and use to cut out two arm cuffs from gold fake leather and the trim from red fake leather. Use the star template on page 173 to cut out the shapes from the red fake leather.

Step 2

Use small pieces of masking tape to hold the trim in place on the bottom and top of each cuff.

Step 3

To stop the fabric sticking while you are sewing, place a piece of tracing paper or baking parchment over the top of the cuff and machine sew the trim in place. Once finished, gently tear off the paper and peel away the masking tape.

Step 4

Glue the stars in the middle of the cuffs using fabric glue.

Step 5

Place one half of the Velcro strip on the back of one of the cuffs at the narrow end, and the other on the front at the other end. Machine sew in place and repeat for the other cuff.

Magic shield

Fend off attacks from evil villains with this simple duct tape shield. Decorate with the symbols used in this book or design your own using any shape and color you prefer.

You will need

3 x 17in (45cm) squares of corrugated cardboard
Scissors
PVA glue
Gold duct tape
12 x 3in (30 x 8cm) strip of blue craft foam
1 x sheet of blue card, 12 x 16in (30 x 40cm)
1 x sheet each of red and yellow card, 8 x 12in
    (20 x 30cm)
Glue stick
Pen or pencil

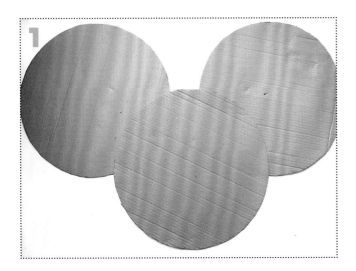

Step 1

Draw a circle about 15in (38cm) in diameter onto one of the squares of corrugated card. Cut out then repeat to make two more cardboard circles.

Step 2

Use PVA glue to fix the three pieces of cardboard together.

Step 3

Cover the edges of the shield with the duct tape by attaching strips of tape approximately 12in (30cm) long along the edge of the shield. Cut vertical snips into the tape down to the shield edge and fold down the tabs to create an even finish.

Step 4

Cover both sides of the shield with long strips of duct tape. Trim the excess tape to create a neat edge around the shield.

Step 5

Draw an 11in (28cm) diameter circle onto blue card and an 8in (20cm) diameter circle onto yellow card, then cut out. Cut out a star shape from red card (use the template on page 173). Glue the larger circle onto the center of the shield, followed by the smaller circle and star on top, using the glue stick. If you like, you can use black and green circles and a lightning shape.

Step 6

To make the handle, take the strip of craft foam and bend it into a C shape. Use duct tape to attach the ends onto the back of the shield in the center.

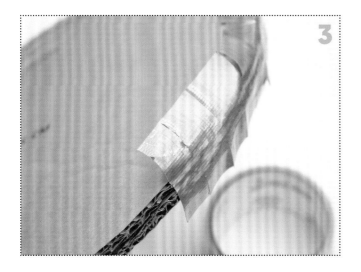

3

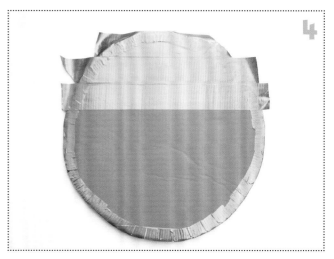

4

5

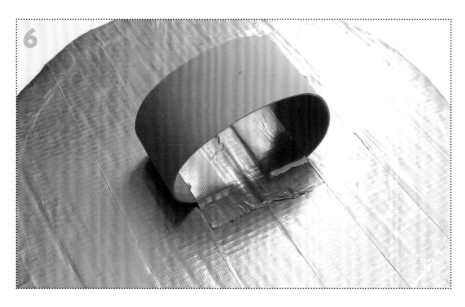

6

Superhero utility belt

This belt is a superhero's best friend, with a hook for a torch and hidden pockets for maps, pens, and money (even superheroes need pocket money!) Large sheets of felt can be purchased from online retailers or good craft stores.

You will need

12 x 40in (30 x 100cm) of thick yellow felt
8½in (22cm) square of bright blue felt
Scissors
Sewing machine and matching thread
Tailor's chalk or pencil
2 x strips of Velcro (hook-and-loop tape),
   3in (8cm) long
Blue carabiner clip

Step 1

Photocopy the belt template on page 173 and cut it out. Fold the yellow felt in half, pin the template on top and draw around it. Extend the sides as long as you need to be able to fit around the child's waist with roughly a 3in (8cm) overlap. Photocopy the belt logo on page 173 and cut out. Cut the belt logo shape out of blue felt. Using the template below, draw and cut your initial letter out of blue felt so that it fits inside the belt logo.

Step 2

Arrange the letter onto the middle of the belt with the blue belt logo on top, then pin in place and machine sew along the edge of the felt.

Step 3

Cut two rectangles measuring 3½ x 5in (9 x 13cm) and a 2½ x 5in (6 x 13cm) triangle from yellow felt. Pin the rectangles on either side of the logo. Machine sew in place around the sides and bottom edge, just inside the edge of the felt, to make pockets. On one of the pockets, sew another line 1½in (4cm) from the side to create a pen holder.

Step 4

Pin the felt triangle at the top of the other pocket, with the base of the triangle ¼in (5mm) from the top of the pocket. The triangle should point down over the pocket, like an envelope. Machine sew along the base of the triangle, making sure you do not stitch over the pocket opening. You now have two pockets, one either side of the emblem.

Step 5

Cut a 2 x ½in (5 x 1cm) strip of yellow felt. Fold it in half and pin to the back of the belt just under one of the pockets. Pin with a ½in (1cm) overlap, with the loop hanging down. Machine sew in place.

Step 6

On the front of the belt, measure and mark with tailor's chalk 2in (5cm) and 5in (13cm) to the left of the envelope pocket, ¾in (2cm) from the top. Repeat for the bottom, ¾in (2cm) up. Do this again on the other side, but this time on the reverse of the belt.

Step 7

At this point check the fit of the utility belt – put it around your child's waist to make sure the fit is within the marks made. If not, expand the marks either side to fit. Take the two strips of Velcro. Pin the fluffy sides onto one side of the belt and the scratchy sides on the other side, between each of the marks. Machine sew in place. Cut away the excess felt on the belt. Attach the carabiner clip to the loop.

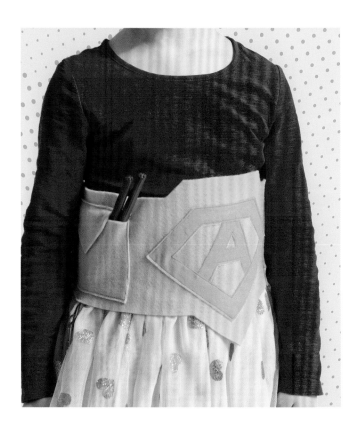

1

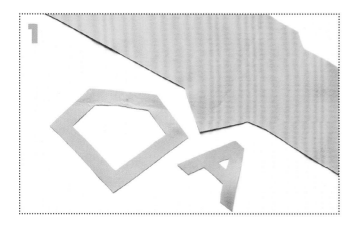

2

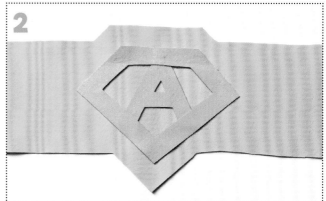

3

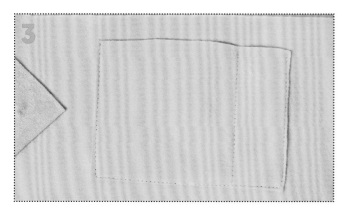

4

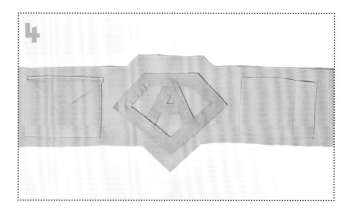

5

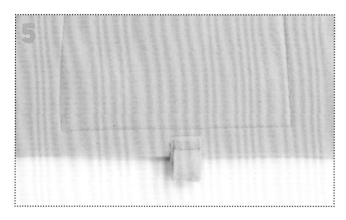

6

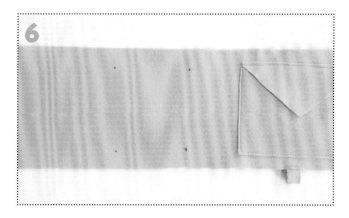

7

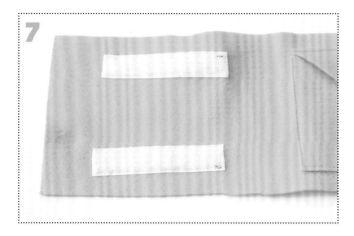

Supersonic car

This car makes the perfect centerpiece for superhero fun. It is made from three large cardboard boxes, but you could use one box and lots of spare card instead. You can paint the car blue like we have here or keep it unpainted. It does require a fair amount of paint – a small pot from a hardware store is a cheaper option than craft paint.

You will need

3 x large cardboard boxes, each about
    18 x 30in (46 x 76cm)
Masking tape
Scissors and craft knife
Tape measure or ruler
Blue and yellow paint
3 x sheets of red card, 8 x 12in (20 x 30cm)
2 x sheets of yellow and black card,
    8 x 12in (20 x 30cm)
1 x sheet of orange card, 8 x 12in (20 x 30cm)
PVA glue
Cardboard tube
A few colorful bottle tops
Acetate, about 17 x 7in (43 x 18cm)

Step 1

Take one of the cardboard boxes and secure all the flaps with masking tape. Using the craft knife, cut down the center of one of the long sides of the box, then cut around the edges, leaving one of the narrow ends attached to create a large flap.

Step 2

Measure about 8in (20cm) from the fold on the flap. Score a line across at this point and fold the cardboard up. Cut out the center of this section, with a 1in (2.5cm) border all the way around, to make the windshield.

Step 3

Cut two right-angle triangles 8 x 6in (20 x 15cm) from spare cardboard. Cut the centers out as before with a 1in (2.5cm) border. Use masking tape to attach these triangles to each side of the windshield and onto the sides of the box.

Step 4

Cut two quarter circles from the cardboard that are the same height as your car. Tape them to the front of the box to make the front panels.

Step 5

Connect the front panels by taping a piece of cardboard, cut to fit, between them. Cut the cardboard so that you can bend it to curve around the panels.

Step 6

Cut two back panels from cardboard, curved upward as shown, and attach to the back of the box in the same way as the front panels. Cut two booster shapes from cardboard and tape inside each back panel.

Step 7

Cut a door into one side of the car, all the way to the bottom and about 12in (30cm) across, making sure you leave one side attached for a hinge. Paint the outside of the car blue, with yellow boosters, and leave to dry. You will probably want to take it outside onto the grass for this bit to avoid mess!

Step 8

Cut a logo from colored card. We've gone for a yellow lightning bolt in a red circle, but you could use your initials or a superhero symbol. Glue onto the side of the car.

Step 9

Cut four wheels from black card. Cut small symbols to match the one on the side of the car. Glue the symbols in the center of the wheels, then glue the wheels onto the car.

Step 10

Cut a sheet of yellow card in half across the width. Curve the edges of the card and glue to the front of the car for headlamps.

Step 11

Cut flames from red and yellow card and glue to the boosters.

Step 12

Cut a piece of acetate to fit the windshield. Cut two lightning bolt shapes from yellow card and glue onto the acetate to make windshield wipers. Glue inside the windshield.

Step 13

Finally, paint a cardboard tube yellow and glue it onto the top of the car door to make a handle. Glue a selection of bottle tops inside the car – you can add labels such as "go" and "stop" if you like.

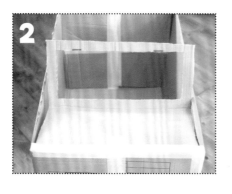

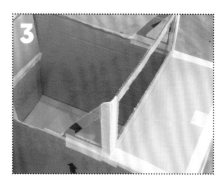

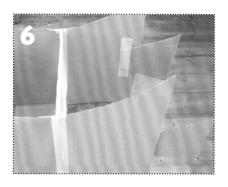

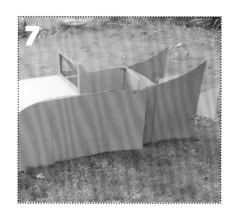

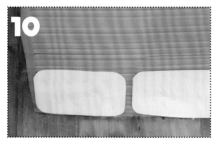

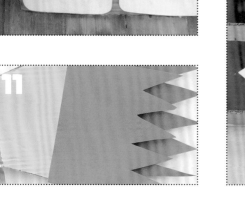

Eye patch and monogrammed hat

No pirate's outfit is complete without an eye patch and hat, and these two are very simple to make from some craft foam and card. Craft foam is a great material to work with, as it's easy to cut out with scissors and is more hard-wearing and water-resistant than card.

You will need

For the eye patch:
3 x 4in (8 x 10cm) black craft foam
3 x 4in (8 x 10cm) white craft foam
Sharp scissors
Hole punch
Pin
Pencil
Strong glue
Sewing needle
12in (30cm) of thin elastic

For the hat:
2 x sheets of black card, 12 x 16in (30 x 40cm)
1 x sheet of white card, 8 x 12in (20 x 30cm)
1 x sheet of black craft foam, 12 x 16in (30 x 40cm)
1 x sheet of gold card, 8 x 12in (20 x 30cm)
Pencil
Scissors or craft knife
Glue stick
Sewing needle
Tape measure
Stapler

Step 1

Photocopy and cut out the templates for the eye patch and the skull and crossbones on page 174. Cut out the eye patch from the black foam and the skull and two bones from the white foam. Use a hole punch to cut out the skull eyes and use a pin to make the nose – give it a wiggle to make it a bit bigger.

Step 2

Arrange the skull and crossbones onto the eye patch as shown in the picture. On one of the bones, mark where it crosses over and cut out the middle section to enable it to lie flat either side of the other bone. Glue in place.

Step 3

Use a needle to pierce the holes on each side of the eye patch, as marked on the template.

Step 4

Thread the elastic through one of the holes, secure with a knot, and trim off any excess. Thread the other end through the other hole, check the fit on your child's head, and knot in place.

Step 5

For the hat, use the template on page 174 to draw and cut out two hat shapes from the black card. Place the template on one half of the card, then flip it over to draw the other half.

Step 6

Use the skull and crossbones template on page 174 to draw and cut out a skull and crossbones from the white card.

Step 7

Draw the child's initials onto a piece of paper (or print them out), no bigger than 2½in (6cm) high, to create a template. Draw around them onto the remaining white card and cut out. Glue the skull and crossbones onto the middle of one of the hat pieces and glue the letters on either side of the skull.

Step 8

Use a tape measure to measure the circumference of your child's head. Cut a 2in (5cm) strip of foam to this length, adding an extra ½in (1cm) for overlap. Staple the two ends together, with the sharp edges of the staples facing out.

Step 9

Staple the foam strip onto the back of one of the hat pieces, at the top and bottom of the foam (again with the sharp edges facing out). Repeat for the other piece, lining up the edges of the card.

Step 10

Staple the side edges of the hat together. Cut the bottom strip off the template and use it as a template to cut two strips of gold card. Arrange along the bottom edge of the hat. Glue in place.

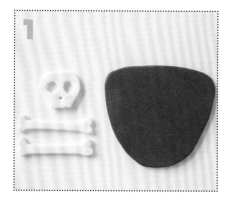

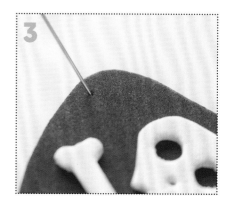

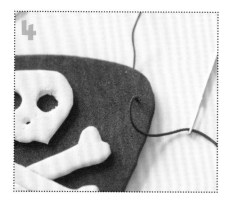

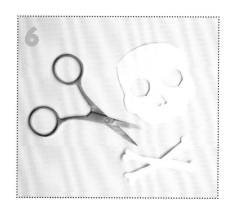

Felt Polly parrot

This pretty Polly makes a great shipmate and a lovely companion for your shoulder. Our parrot has been made with a sewing machine, but she can easily be stitched by hand instead. Felt is a great material to work with – it's brightly colored, inexpensive, and the edges don't fray. Polly is compatible with the waistcoat on page 146, or with a little Velcro (hook-and-loop tape) you can create a perch for her on any top.

You will need

1 x sheet each of yellow, red and blue felt,
    8 x 12in (20 x 30cm)
Scraps of black and white felt
Handful of toy stuffing
Scissors
Red, yellow, white, and blue sewing thread,
    pins and sewing machine
Yellow and black embroidery thread
Embroidery needle
1½in (4cm) loop-side piece of sew-on Velcro
    (hook-and-loop tape)

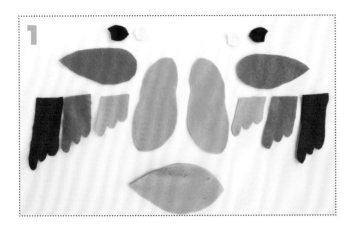

Step 1
Photocopy and cut out the templates on page 174, then cut the following pieces from felt:
2 x body pieces in yellow felt
2 x wing pieces in blue felt
2 x eye pieces in white felt
2 x beak pieces in black felt
1 x belly piece in yellow felt
2 x outer tail feathers in red felt
2 x middle tail feathers in blue felt
2 x inner tail feathers in yellow felt

Step 2
To create Polly's tail feathers, use contrasting thread to sew two rows of equally spaced stitches along the length of each feather.

Step 3
Layer the feathers together with the big feather at the bottom and the smallest at the top, and line up the top edges. Pin and sew together ¼in (6mm) from the top. Repeat for the other set of feathers, making sure the two sets are mirror images of each other.

Step 4
Sew the tail feathers onto the body piece along the existing stitch line at the top of the feathers. See the photo for where to place the feathers. Pin the wings onto the body piece above the feathers so the top of the feathers are under the wings and sew along the top curved edge.

Step 5
Pin and sew a white eye piece onto both of the body pieces using white thread. Pin each beak piece onto the inside of the body pieces with a ¼in (6mm) overlap and sew using yellow thread.

Step 6
Use black embroidery thread to hand sew an eye onto the middle of the white eye piece; sew overlapping crosses to create a star.

Step 7
Pin the belly piece to one of the body pieces with the edges lined up and use yellow embroidery thread to hand stitch the two pieces together using blanket stitch (see page 57 for stitch instructions).

Step 8
Pin and stitch the other body piece to the other side of the belly piece with the edges lined up again. Stitch the two body pieces together where they meet, stopping once you reach the beak.

Step 9
Fill the parrot with stuffing until she is plump. Use black embroidery thread to blanket stitch the beak together neatly. Sew a square of Velcro to Polly's bottom to enable her to perch on the Easy-sew waistcoat (see page 146).

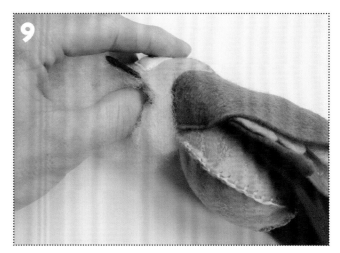

First mate's telescope

Ahoy! Pirates will easily be able to spot enemy ships with this cardboard tube telescope, which makes it one of the most important pieces of equipment on board any pirate ship. This telescope is extra special because it comes complete with its own seascape drawn inside.

You will need

1 x cardboard cup, about 4½ x 3½in (11 x 9cm)
1 x cardboard tube, about 4½ x 2in (11 x 5cm)
1 x sheet of acetate, about 3in (8cm) square
1 x sheet of gold card, 8 x 12in (20 x 30cm)
Permanent markers in a range of colors
Craft knife
Black paint and paintbrush
Strong glue
Masking tape

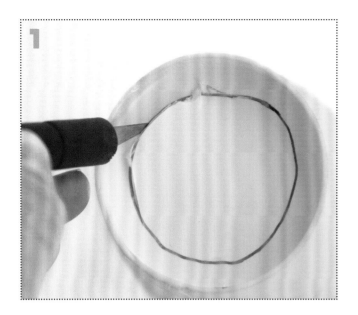

Step 1

Begin by drawing a circle on the bottom of the cup ¼in (6mm) in from the rim. Use a craft knife to cut this out.

Step 2

Paint the inside of the cup and cardboard tube black and leave to dry. You may need several coats to get an even coverage.

Step 3

On your sheet of acetate, draw around the end of the tube and cut out. Draw a little seascape image onto the acetate circle using permanent markers.

Step 4

Use strong glue to stick the seascape inside the bottom of the cup. Leave to dry.

Step 5

Use masking tape to attach the tube onto the bottom of the cup.

Step 6

Paint the outside of the telescope black and leave to dry.

Step 7

Cut three ½in (1cm) wide strips of gold card long enough to fit around the top, middle and bottom of the telescope (with a slight overlap). Glue in place on the telescope.

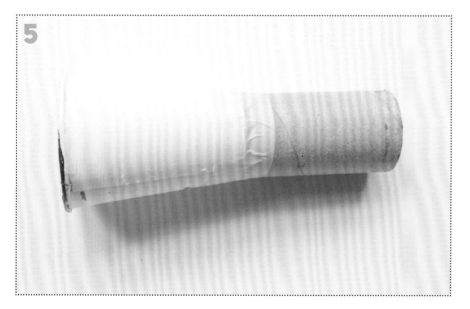

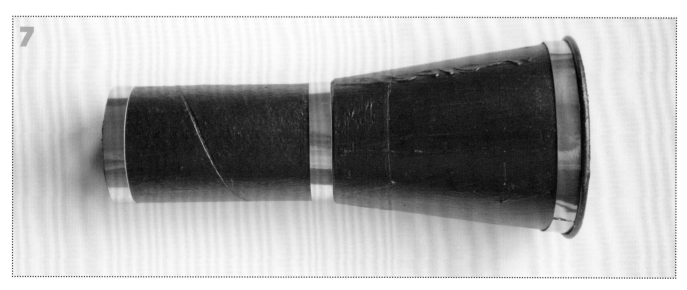

Captain's hook

This pirate hook is made using the end of a plastic bottle, wire, and duct tape. It has a handle on the inside so that children can hold onto it and cover their hand.

You will need

Wire coat hanger
3½-pint (2-liter) plastic bottle
Handful of moldable clay
3 or 4 large sheets of newspaper
Craft foam
Wire cutters
Marker pen
Scissors
Masking tape
PVA glue
Silver duct tape
Paintbrush
Red and black paints
Tape measure
Pencil

Step 1
First, cut off the hook from the coat hanger. Mark a line 2in (5cm) from the center of the hanger on both sides and use wire cutters to cut it off. Twist the two ends together.

Step 2
Discard the lid from the plastic bottle and mark 5in (13cm) down from the rim. Draw a line all around the bottle at this point and use scissors to cut along it.

Step 3
Fill the neck of the bottle with moldable clay and push the coat hanger through the top. Just the hook part should be visible through the top of the bottle, with the rest of the wire inside (this will be used as the handle).

Step 4
Use masking tape to cover the top and bottom of the bottle top to keep the hook in place.

Step 5
Make up some papier-mâché paste by mixing two parts PVA to one part water and then tearing up pieces of newspaper to make roughly 1in (2.5cm) squares.

Step 6
Spread glue onto the plastic bottle and place the newspaper pieces on top. Then spread glue on top of the newspaper and cover the inside and outside of the hook, making sure there are no gaps.

Step 7
Draw around the hook onto the foam, adding ¼in (6mm) onto either side. Repeat this to create two foam hooks, then place them on either side of the wire hook and tape in place with silver duct tape.

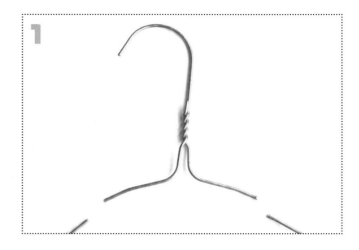

Step 8
Paint the base of the hook red.

Step 9
Once dry, measure ½in (1cm) from the bottom and use a tape measure and pencil to mark a line all the way around. Add three more lines, each ¼in (6mm) above the previous, in order to create two stripes.

Step 10
Carefully paint the stripes black.

Step 11
For decoration, use the black paint to create small triangles just under the neck of the bottle.

Step 12
Finally, wrap duct tape around the wire in the center of the bottle several times to create a comfortable padded handle.

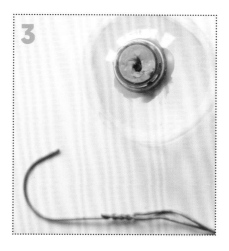

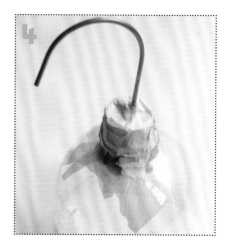

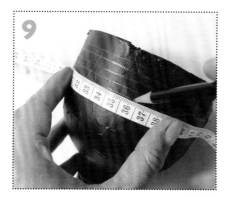

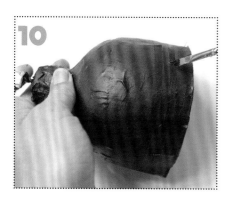

Buccaneer boots

These boots are an easy upcycling project using a pair of old wellies covered with black duct tape and a gold buckle. You could use black wellies if you have them without duct tape, but the embellishments are less likely to stick – and they will still tend to look like wellies at the end!

You will need

Pair of wellington boots
1 sheet of black craft foam, 12 x 16in (30 x 40cm)
47in (120cm) of ¼in (6mm)-thick red ribbon
Scraps of gold craft foam
Roll of 2in (5cm)-wide duct tape
Scissors
Pencil
Single hole punch
Double-sided tape

Step 1
Wrap a strip of duct tape over the toe end of the boots. Pinch the excess corners of tape together tightly and snip them off to create a neat edge.

Step 2
Continue to cover the boots with the tape – cut small slits around any curved parts if the duct tape doesn't sit flat.

Step 3
For the top of the boots, add a strip of tape around the top that sits halfway above the edge of the boot.

Step 4
Cut slits into the excess tape, fold it over and press inside the boot.

Step 5
Use the template on page 174 to cut out two black foam cuffs. Make two pencil marks on each end, ½in (1cm) from the edge and ½in (1cm) from both the top and bottom. Use a hole punch to make a hole through each mark.

Step 6
Use double-sided tape to attach the foam cuff to the top of the boots, with the top edges lined up. The ends should meet at the back.

Step 7
Cut the ribbon in half and thread it through the holes in the cuff like a shoelace. Tie in a bow to secure.

Step 8
For the straps, cut two strips of foam measuring 10 x 1½in (25 x 4cm). Trim one end on each piece to create a curved edge. Use the hole punch to make four holes, about ½in (1cm) from the edge and ½in (1cm) apart.

Step 9
Cut two buckle shapes from gold craft foam using the template on page 174. Slide them onto the strap about ¾in (2cm) from the end. Use double-sided tape to attach the straps around the top of the foot of the boot, with the buckles on the outside over the ankle.

Cutlass and belt

This sturdy cardboard cutlass is great for fending off pesky rival pirates trying to steal treasure. It comes with a handy fabric belt to hold the cutlass.

You will need

2 x pieces of corrugated card, about
    18in (45cm) square
15in (38cm) of 1/16in (1.5mm)-thick wire
About 11ft (3.3m) of green string
Scrap of fabric for belt (see Step 8 for
    measurements)
1 x gold button, ¾in (2cm) in diameter
Marker pen

Scissors
Strong glue
Silver duct tape
Wire cutters
Black duct tape
Double-sided tape
Sewing machine, matching thread and pins
Iron and ironing board
Sewing needle

Step 1

Place the template from page 174 onto the corrugated card, draw around it and cut it out. Repeat to create two cutlass shapes.

Step 2

Spread glue onto one of the pieces of card and glue the other one on top. Leave to dry.

Step 3

Place a strip of silver duct tape along the long edge of the cutlass. Cut small tabs, 1in (2.5cm) apart, along the edge of the tape and fold over; the tabs will prevent the tape from puckering around the curved edge. Repeat for all the other edges.

Step 4

Attach strips of duct tape down the front and back of the cutlass and trim off any excess from the edges.

Step 5

Use wire cutters to wrap the end of the wire twice around the handle to secure it in place, 1in (2.5cm) from the end. Bend it over and wrap it around again, about 4in (10cm) from where you started. Snip off the excess wire, then cover with silver duct tape where it folds over the card to conceal any sharp edges.

Step 6

Wrap black duct tape all the way around the wire handle.

Step 7

Wrap double-sided tape around the cutlass in between the handle. Peel off the backing and wrap the green string over the tape, nice and tightly. Put a dab of strong glue onto both ends of the string to secure it in place.

Step 8

Measure your child's waist for the belt. The belt should hang loosely, so take this into account when taking the measurement. Add an extra 2in (5cm) to this measurement. Cut a 6in (15cm)-wide strip of fabric to this length.

Step 9

Fold the fabric in half lengthways. Pin and sew along the edge with a ½in (1cm) seam allowance. Turn the fabric the right way out and press with the seam running down the center.

Step 10

Turn under each end by ½in (1cm). Pin and sew just inside the fold to hide the raw edges.

Step 11

Sew the button onto the belt, 1in (2.5cm) from one end. Then mark a buttonhole 1in (2.5cm) from the opposite end and cut a slit the same length as the button. Sew the buttonhole by machine or hand. To hand sew, carefully blanket stitch (see page 57) around the raw edges.

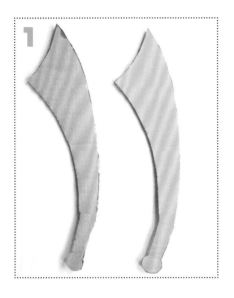

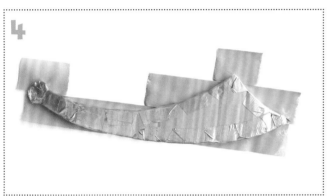

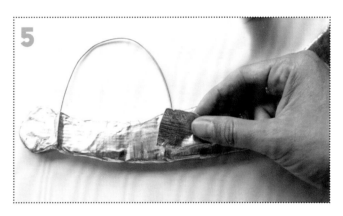

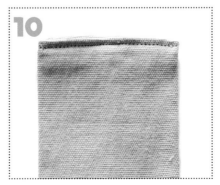

Easy-sew waistcoat

This little waistcoat is a one-size-fits-all (all kids, that is!) super-easy sewing project. Bias binding is added to finish the edges. Adding binding to the tuck on the back can be a little fiddly, so if you are a novice sewer follow the dotted line on the template to avoid the tuck. Pair with a stripy T-shirt for the best pirate effect.

You will need

20in (50cm) square of black cotton fabric
13ft (4m) of red bias binding tape
About 12in (30cm) square of fusible webbing
About 12in (30cm) square of white cotton
6 x gold buttons, ¾in (2cm) in diameter
Scissors
Sewing machine, matching thread and pins
Iron and ironing board
Pencil
Tape measure
Optional: 1½in (4cm) hook-side piece of sew-on
    black Velcro (hook-and-loop tape)

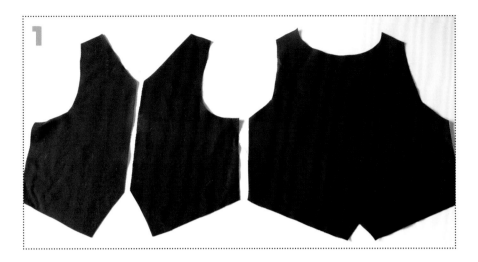

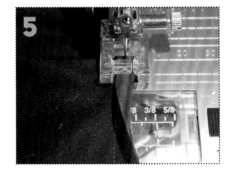

Step 1

Cut out the pattern pieces from page 175. Fold the fabric and use the pattern to cut out two front pieces and one back piece from the black fabric. Place the back piece along the fold of the fabric where indicated.

Step 2

Pin the front and back pieces together at the shoulders and side seams and sew with a ½in (1cm) seam allowance.

Step 3

Open up the bias binding and line up the edge with the bottom of the waistcoat, on the wrong side of the fabric.

Step 4

Pin all the way along, going round the tuck in the center if you have opted to sew it (this is a little fiddly) to the end. Sew along the fold in the binding.

Step 5

Fold the binding over the fabric, then pin and sew in place on the right side of the waistcoat along the center of the binding. The binding should enclose the raw edges of the fabric.

Step 6

Repeat for the side panels – start from one bottom corner of the waistcoat and sew all the way around the neckline to the other corner.

Step 7

Trim the edges of the binding when you reach the other side so that it is neat against the bottom.

Step 8

Repeat for the armholes, leaving ½in (1cm) excess at the end of the binding to overlap a little.

Step 9

Iron the fusible webbing onto the white fabric to glue them together. Use the template on page 175 to cut two bone shapes from the fabric. Remove the backing from the webbing and line up to form a cross on the back of the waistcoat. Iron this in place.

Step 10

Measure and mark in pencil three evenly spaced points along both sides of the waistcoat, ¾in (2cm) from the edge. Sew the gold buttons in place. If you want to create a perch for Felt Polly parrot (see page 126), sew a square of Velcro onto one shoulder.

Pirate ship

There are many ways to build a boat, and you can adapt yours to suit the materials you have available. The more boxes you can find, the bigger your boat can be, and the more shipmates you can fit on deck. Bear in mind, though, that the boat will decrease in sturdiness the bigger it gets!

You will need

3–4 large cardboard boxes and scraps
    of corrugated card
Yogurt pot or large plastic lid
Paper plates
Sheets of acetate
Selection of bottle tops for buttons
Broom handle or long length of dowel
Terracotta plant pot with a hole in the base for
    the broom handle or piece of dowel
Bunting and old sheets for sail and sea

Felt
Colorful duct tape
Scissors and craft knife
Strong glue
Felt-tip pens
Gold and silver acrylic paints
    and paintbrushes
Laundry detergent bottle lid
Large dinner plate

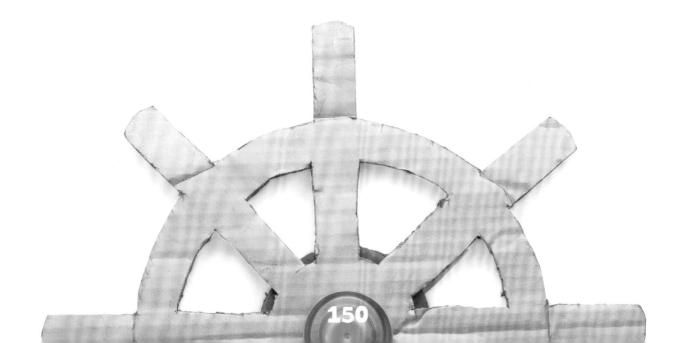

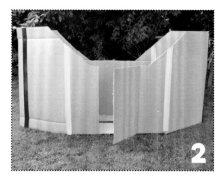

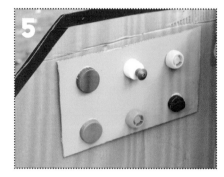

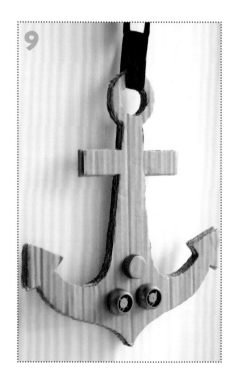

Step 1

Cut open two or three large cardboard boxes, then reassemble them to form a ship shape with narrower pointed ends. Tape in place with plenty of duct tape.

Step 2

Cut a door into one side of the boat. Add a handle by sticking on a yoghurt pot or large lid (laundry detergent lids work well).

Step 3

To be able to fold the boat away for storage, make the base as a separate section that can be pulled out when playtime is over. You can draw around the boat onto a large sheet of card (or several smaller ones taped together) and cut this out.

Step 4

Portholes can be made by cutting holes in the side of the box, just smaller than a paper plate. For each porthole, cut away the center of a paper plate and replace with a piece of acetate to look like glass. Glue this onto the holes and decorate with bolts using felt-tip pens.

Step 5

Bottle tops of all shapes and sizes make great buttons for a control panel. Ones with flip-up caps or twisting nozzles work best for playing with. Stick them onto a small piece of cardboard and attach inside the boat.

Step 6

To create a plank, cut a long strip of cardboard and tape it inside the boat, coming out through the door. It can then be folded up inside the boat when not in use.

Step 7

A broom handle or long piece of dowel sitting inside an upturned terracotta plant pot makes an excellent mast. It can be adorned with bunting or an old sheet for a sail.

Step 8

Surround the boat with an old blue bedsheet to create the sea. Cut shark fins or crocodiles from cardboard and throw them into the sea to create infested waters.

Step 9

To make an anchor, cut out two anchor shapes from corrugated card and glue them together. Glue on bottle tops, painted gold or copper as decoration. Make a chain by gluing or sewing strips of felt into loops in a chain, then glue the chain onto the boat.

Step 10

Make a helm for your ship by drawing around a large dinner plate onto a piece of corrugated card. Draw another circle, 1½in (4cm) smaller, inside. Add 1½in (4cm) wide strips of card across the circles to create handles – they should come about 4in (10cm) out from the edge of the circle. Cut out and paint silver. Draw around a large laundry detergent bottle lid (one with an inner and outer rim) in the center and cut out, then insert the lid through the middle of the wheel and glue onto the boat. The wheel should spin freely around the lid.

Mermaid blanket

Get warm, snug, and ready listen to aquatic tales (or tails!) with this cozy fleece mermaid tail blanket. The blanket should be long enough to reach to your child's chest – this one, made for a five-year-old, is 40in (1m) long. You will need a sewing machine for this project.

You will need

80in (2m) of dark purple fleece
60in (1.5m) of pale purple fleece
40in (1m) of pink fleece
Scissors
Pins
Tailor's chalk
Sewing machine
Coordinating sewing thread and lighter color
     sewing thread

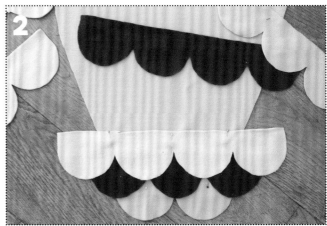

Step 1

Using the diagram on page 175 as a guide, draw out the body of the blanket onto the piece of dark purple fleece, using tailor's chalk. Cut it out, then cut out another identical piece from pale purple fleece. Using the diagram as a guide, draw and cut out the fin from the dark purple fleece.

Step 2

Use the template on page 175 to cut rows of scales from each color of fleece. Vary the size of the rows to fit across the blanket at each point. Start at the bottom and pin the scales onto the front piece, overlapping the scales and alternating colors as you work your way up.

Step 3

Starting from the bottom, sew along the top straight edge of the scales, moving the overlapping scales out of the way as you go. Repeat to sew all the scales in place.

Step 4

Trim the excess scales off the sides of the blanket, following the line of the main piece underneath.

Step 5

Cut two strips of dark purple fleece measuring 4 x 30in (10 x 75cm). Fold and pin one strip over the top of the scaled blanket piece to conceal the raw edges. Sew ¼in (5mm) in from the edge of the strip. Repeat for the plain blanket piece.

Step 6

Pin the blanket pieces right sides together. Sew along both sides with a 1in (2.5cm) seam allowance. Trim the excess fabric. Keep the bottom of the blanket open.

Step 7

Use the tailor's chalk to mark decorative lines onto the tail fin. Sew over the lines using a lighter color of thread.

Step 8

Sandwich the tail fin into the bottom of the blanket, with an overlap of 1in (2.5cm). Lift the bottom row of scales out of the way, then sew from the top of the blanket, with a ½in (1cm) seam allowance.

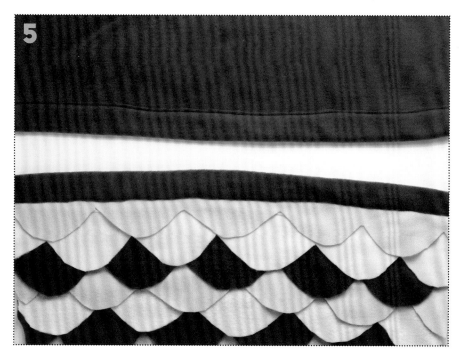

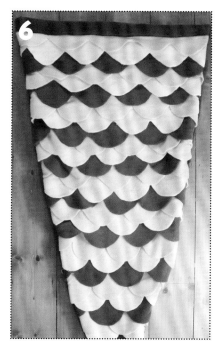

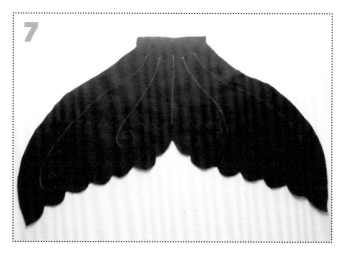

Shell necklace

No mermaid is fully dressed without a pretty shell necklace. This one is made from cardboard tubes, paper plates, and paper, so it's probably not a good idea to go swimming in the sea while you're wearing it!

You will need

Scissors
2 x cardboard tubes
1 x paper plate
PVA glue
String
1 x sheet of white paper, 8 x 12in (20 x 30cm)
Pencil and ruler
Wooden skewer
Parchment paper
Pearlescent pink and green paints,
    yellow paint, and paintbrush
Selection of stick-on pearls in different sizes
Tweezers (optional)
About 30in (80cm) of fine elastic
Small plastic beads

Step 3

To make the paper beads, use a pencil and a ruler to draw triangles right across the length of the paper. The triangles should measure 1½in (4cm) at the widest end. Cut these triangles out. You will need about eight.

Step 4

To turn the triangles into beads, spread glue on one side of the paper, leaving 1in (2.5cm) unglued at the wider end. Place a skewer at this end and slowly roll up the paper around it. Remove the skewer and place the bead on parchment paper to dry.

Step 5

Paint the shells – pearlescent paint creates a pretty effect. To create an ombré effect, paint the top of the shell one color and the bottom another color. Mix the paint a little on a palette and dab it onto the shell so that the colors blend.

Step 1

Use the templates on page 175 to cut out the shell shapes. Cut two small and two medium shells from a cardboard tube. Cut the large shell from a paper plate, lining up the bottom of the shell with the ridged edge of the plate.

Step 2

Cover one of the shells with glue. Add a line of string down the center and bend it back round leaving a ¼in (6mm) loop for hanging at the base. Add string to the rest of the shell to resemble ridges, as shown in the picture. When the glue has dried, trim off any excess string.

Step 6

Paint the paper beads to match the necklace and leave to dry.

Step 7

Add a few pearls to the bottom of each shell. If you have tweezers, use them to pick up the pearls, dip them in glue, and place them onto the shells. Leave the glue to dry.

Step 8

Thread the shells onto the elastic, along with the paper beads and the plastic beads, in whichever design you like. Here we have put the largest shell in the center with the smaller shells on the outside. Measure the necklace around your neck to work out the sizing, then tie the elastic and trim the excess.

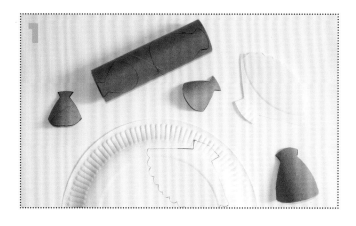

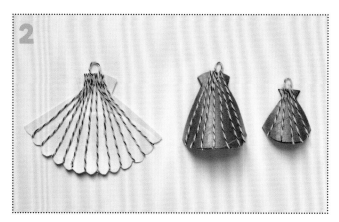

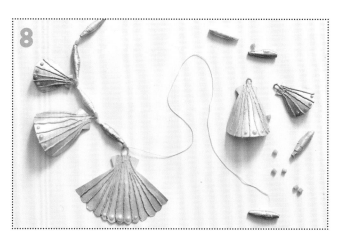

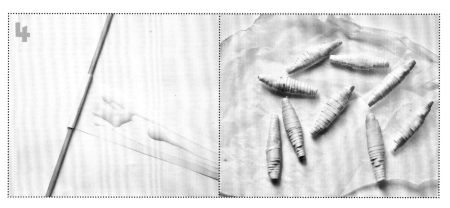

Triton's crown and spear

All rulers of the sea need a crown and spear to complete their royal aquatic duties. Kids will love getting their hands messy helping with the papier-mâché for these brilliant makes. Bear in mind that the crown and spear will need time to dry, so this project should be made over two sessions.

You will need

2 x pieces of corrugated card, about 25 x 30in (65 x 90cm)
Scissors
Masking tape
3 x sheets of craft foam (any color), 6 x 8in (15 x 20cm)
PVA glue
2 or 3 sheets of newspaper
Gold paint and paintbrush
Selection of shells in various sizes
Selection of gems and pearls in various sizes and colors
About 40in (1m) of string

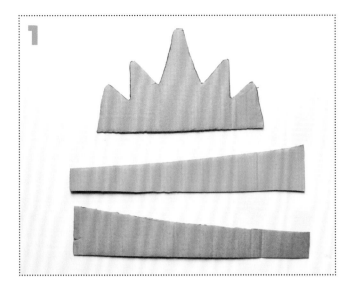

Step 1
Use the template on page 175 to cut out the front section of the crown from corrugated card. Cut two strips of card measuring roughly 2in (5cm) wide and long enough to wrap around a child's head with a slight overlap. The strips can taper slightly if you wish.

Step 2
Attach the strips to each side of the crown with masking tape. Curve them round with your fingers.

Step 3
Cover the inside and outside of the crown with craft foam. Glue the foam on and cut it to the shape of the crown. Test the crown on your child's head for size. Fix it together with masking tape.

Step 4
Place the template from page 175 at the top of the corrugated card, leaving room for the handle. Draw around it and add a handle measuring about 2 x 18in (5 x 45cm). Cut it out and use this to draw another spear on the other piece of card, as it needs to be double thickness.

Step 5
Glue the spear pieces together. Cover the front, back, and sides in craft foam as with the crown.

Step 6
Make the papier-mâché paste by mixing two parts PVA glue to one part water. Tear newspaper into small pieces and cover the crown and spear completely on all sides. Leave to dry overnight and apply a second coat of paste. When the papier-mâché is dry, paint it gold.

Step 7
Take a selection of shells and gems and stick them onto the front of the crown and spear in a design you like.

Step 8
Paint the string gold and leave it to dry. Arrange it around the bottom of the crown so that it hangs down like chains. Cut and glue in place.

3

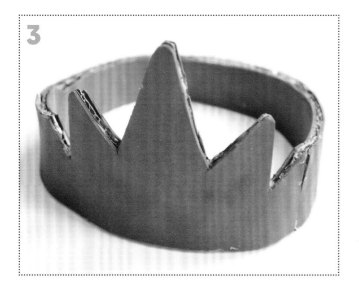

4

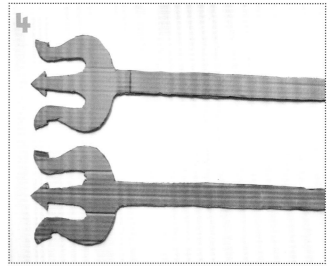

5

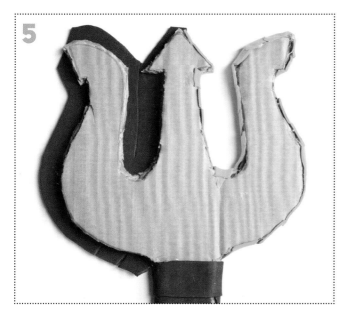

6

7

8

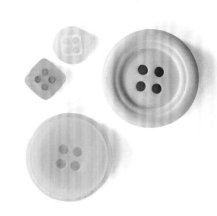

Button art T-shirt

This is a really easy craft that kids can happily get involved with. They will love to see the shape evolving from the buttons. You don't have to do a mermaid tail, you could do anything you like – a seahorse, shell, waves or any other shape as long as it is not too complicated.

You will need

Tailor's chalk or pencil
Plain cotton T-shirt
2 handfuls of pastel-colored buttons
White sewing thread
Sewing needle
Embroidery hoop (optional)
Blue embroidery thread
Letter-size/A4 piece of paper
　　or card
Tweezers
Stick-on pearls
Fabric glue

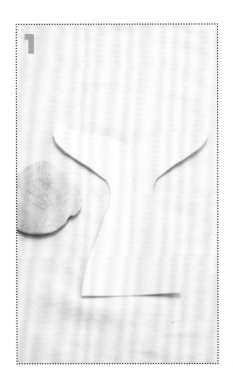

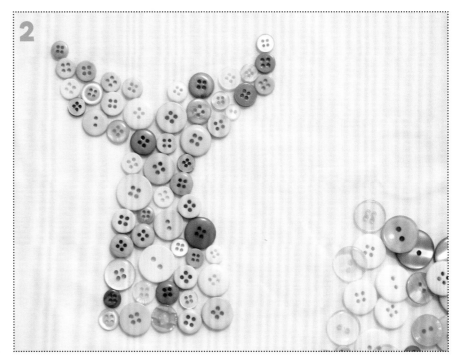

Step 1

Use the template on page 175 to draw a mermaid tail onto a piece of paper. Use tailor's chalk or a pencil to draw around the tail onto the middle of the T-shirt, with the fin at the top. If you're using pencil, draw a very light line.

Step 2

Remove the paper and arrange the buttons roughly within the tail outline on the T-shirt. If you like, you can take a picture to use in the next step for reference.

Step 3

Stitch the buttons in place by hand. If you have one, use an embroidery hoop to make the sewing easier.

Step 4

Remove the hoop if using. Don't worry if there are any gaps, as they will be filled in with pearls.

Step 5

Use tailor's chalk or pencil to draw a few wavy ocean lines at the bottom of the tail. Use blue embroidery thread to backstitch the lines in.

Step 6

Place a piece of card inside the T-shirt to protect the back. Fill any gaps in the tail with the pearls, fixing them with fabric glue. To make it easier, you can use tweezers to pick up the pearls, dip them in glue, and place them onto the T-shirt.

3

4

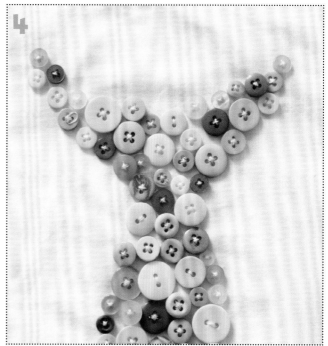

5

6

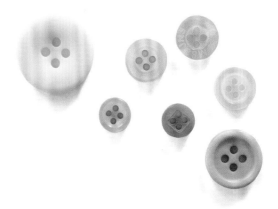

Templates

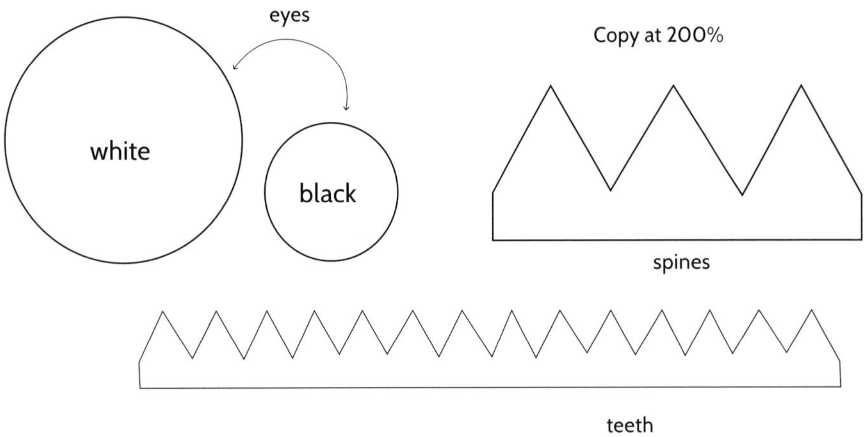

eyes

white

black

Copy at 200%

spines

teeth

Spiny dino cape (see page 22)

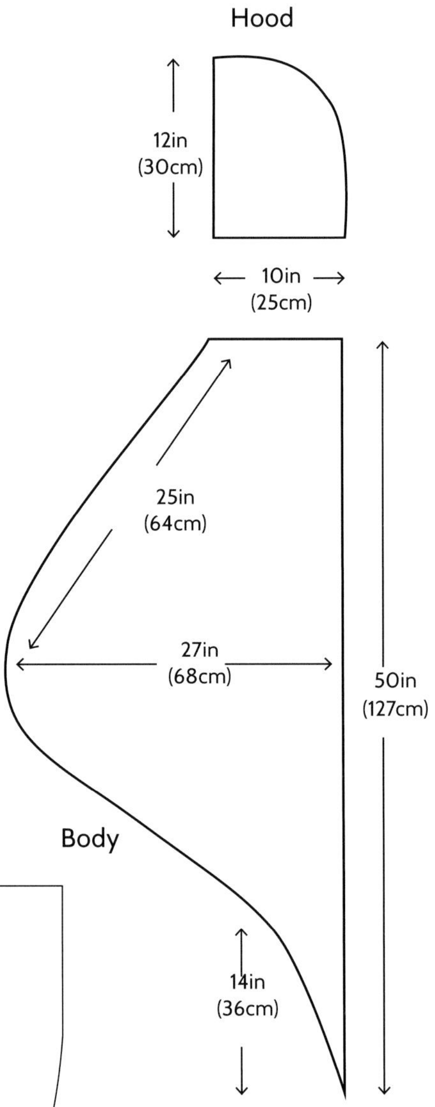

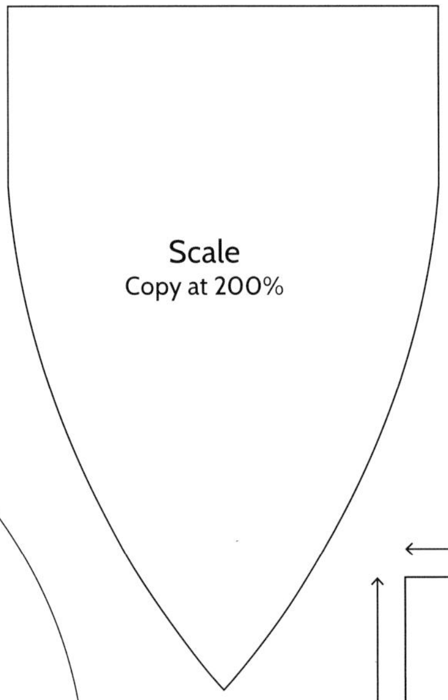

Hood

12in
(30cm)

10in
(25cm)

25in
(64cm)

27in
(68cm)

50in
(127cm)

14in
(36cm)

Body

Foot cover

Dinosaur paws
(see page 14)

Copy at 300%

Paw

Claw

Scale
Copy at 200%

Pterodactyl wings
(see page 18)

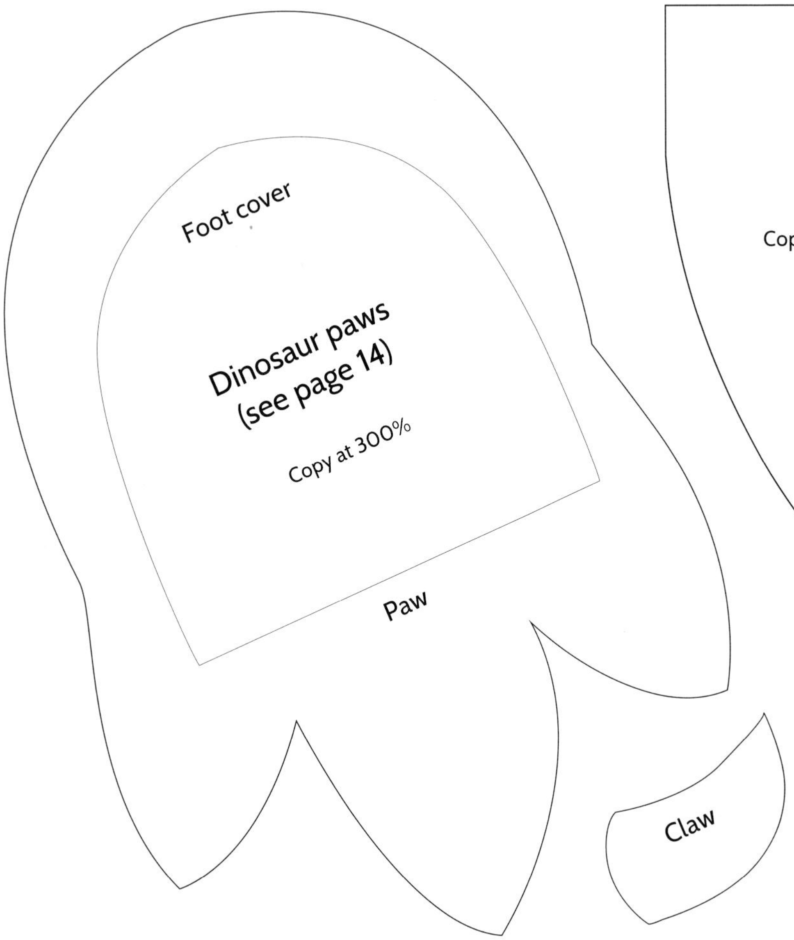

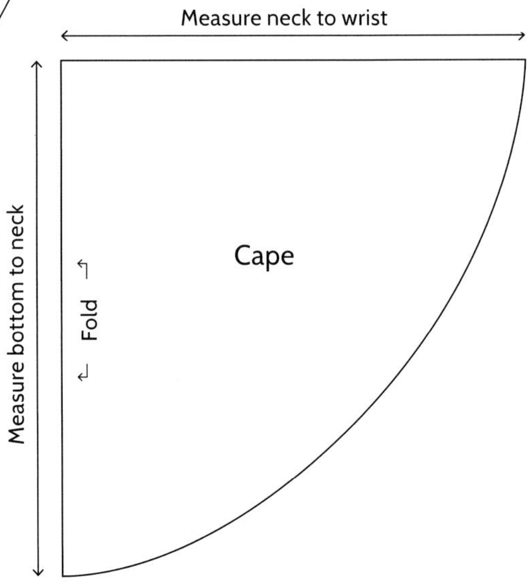

Measure neck to wrist

Measure bottom to neck

Fold

Cape

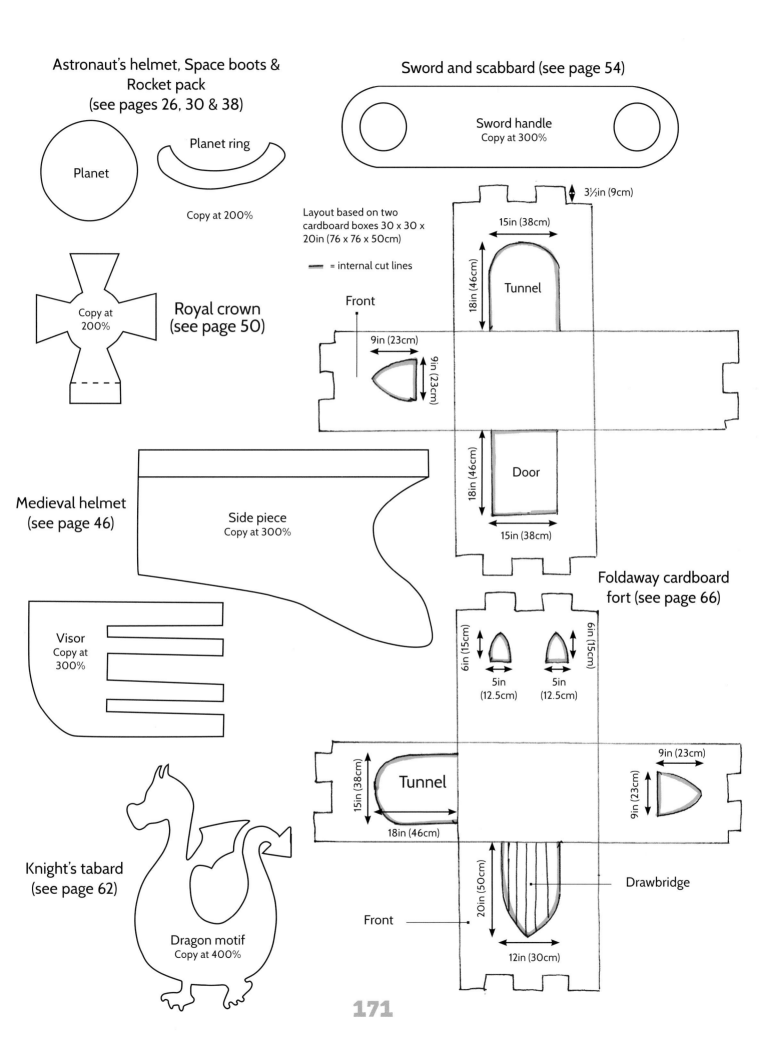

Astronaut's helmet, Space boots &
Rocket pack
(see pages 26, 30 & 38)

Planet

Planet ring

Copy at 200%

Copy at 200%

Royal crown
(see page 50)

Medieval helmet
(see page 46)

Side piece
Copy at 300%

Visor
Copy at
300%

Knight's tabard
(see page 62)

Dragon motif
Copy at 400%

Sword and scabbard (see page 54)

Sword handle
Copy at 300%

Layout based on two
cardboard boxes 30 x 30 x
20in (76 x 76 x 50cm)

= internal cut lines

Front

3½in (9cm)

15in (38cm)

18in (46cm)

Tunnel

9in (23cm)

9in (23cm)

18in (46cm)

Door

15in (38cm)

Foldaway cardboard
fort (see page 66)

6in (15cm)

6in (15cm)

5in
(12.5cm)

5in
(12.5cm)

15in (38cm)

Tunnel

18in (46cm)

9in (23cm)

9in (23cm)

20in (50cm)

Drawbridge

Front

12in (30cm)

171

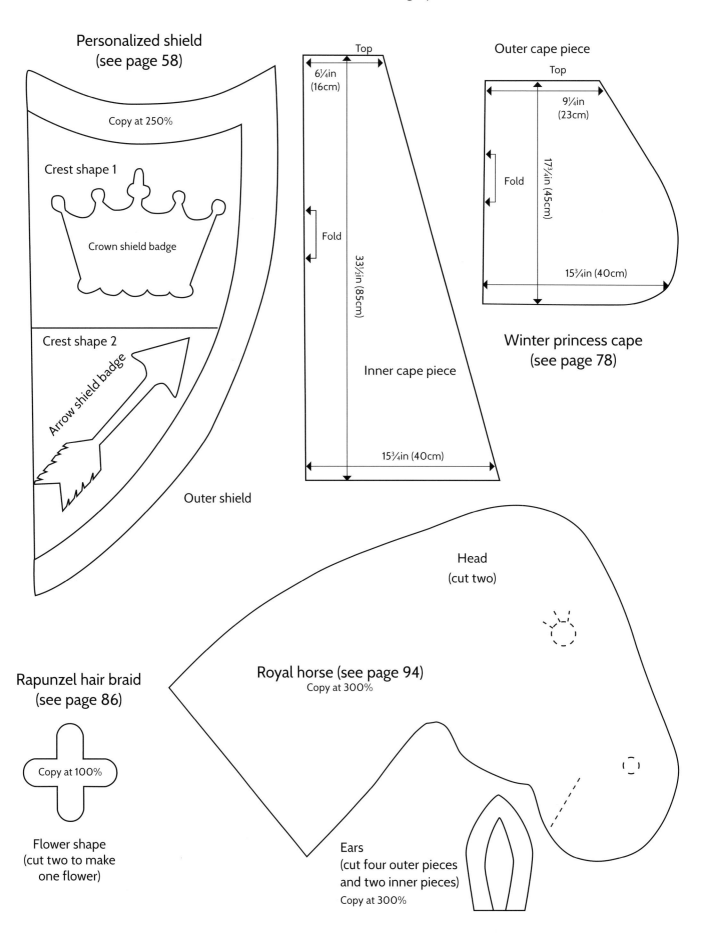

Personalized shield
(see page 58)

Copy at 250%

Crest shape 1

Crown shield badge

Crest shape 2

Arrow shield badge

Outer shield

Top

6¼in
(16cm)

Fold

33½in (85cm)

15¾in (40cm)

Inner cape piece

Outer cape piece

Top

9¼in
(23cm)

Fold

17¾in (45cm)

15¾in (40cm)

Winter princess cape
(see page 78)

Head
(cut two)

Royal horse (see page 94)
Copy at 300%

Rapunzel hair braid
(see page 86)

Copy at 100%

Flower shape
(cut two to make
one flower)

Ears
(cut four outer pieces
and two inner pieces)
Copy at 300%

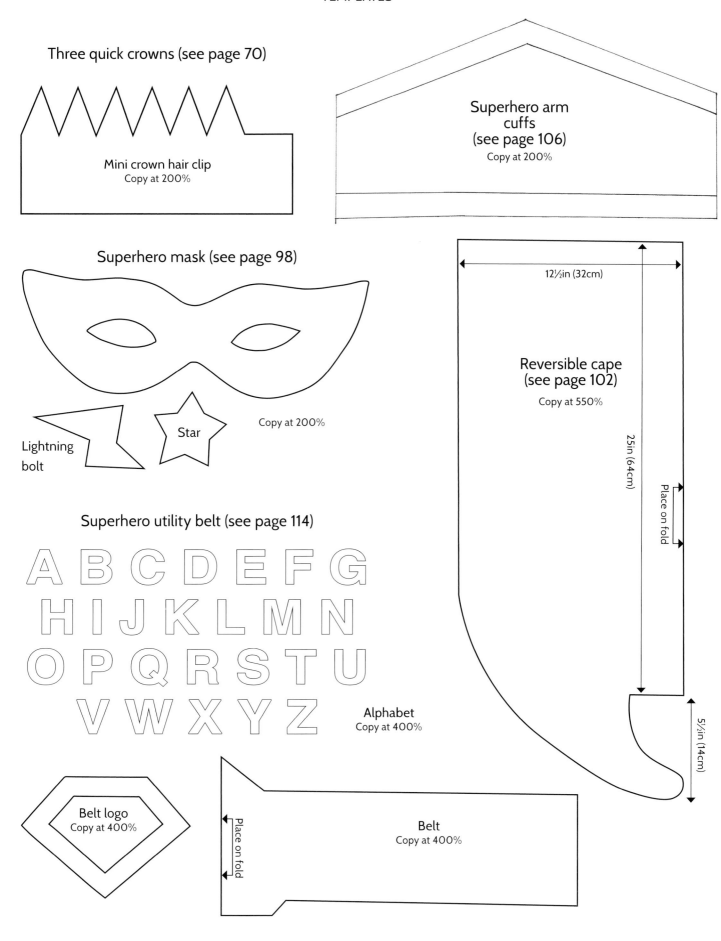

Three quick crowns (see page 70)

Mini crown hair clip
Copy at 200%

Superhero arm
cuffs
(see page 106)
Copy at 200%

Superhero mask (see page 98)

Copy at 200%

Lightning
bolt

Star

Reversible cape
(see page 102)

Copy at 550%

12½in (32cm)

25in (64cm)

Place on fold

5½in (14cm)

Superhero utility belt (see page 114)

A B C D E F G
H I J K L M N
O P Q R S T U
V W X Y Z

Alphabet
Copy at 400%

Belt logo
Copy at 400%

Place on fold

Belt
Copy at 400%

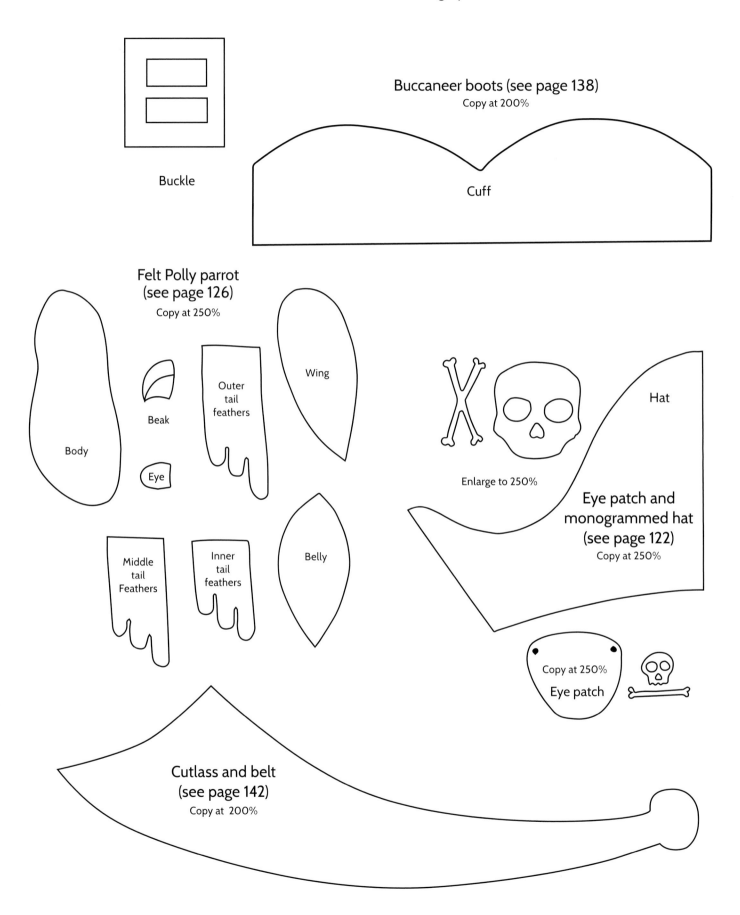

Buckle

Buccaneer boots (see page 138)
Copy at 200%

Cuff

Felt Polly parrot
(see page 126)
Copy at 250%

Body

Beak

Eye

Outer
tail
feathers

Wing

Middle
tail
Feathers

Inner
tail
feathers

Belly

Enlarge to 250%

Hat

Eye patch and
monogrammed hat
(see page 122)
Copy at 250%

Copy at 250%
Eye patch

Cutlass and belt
(see page 142)
Copy at 200%

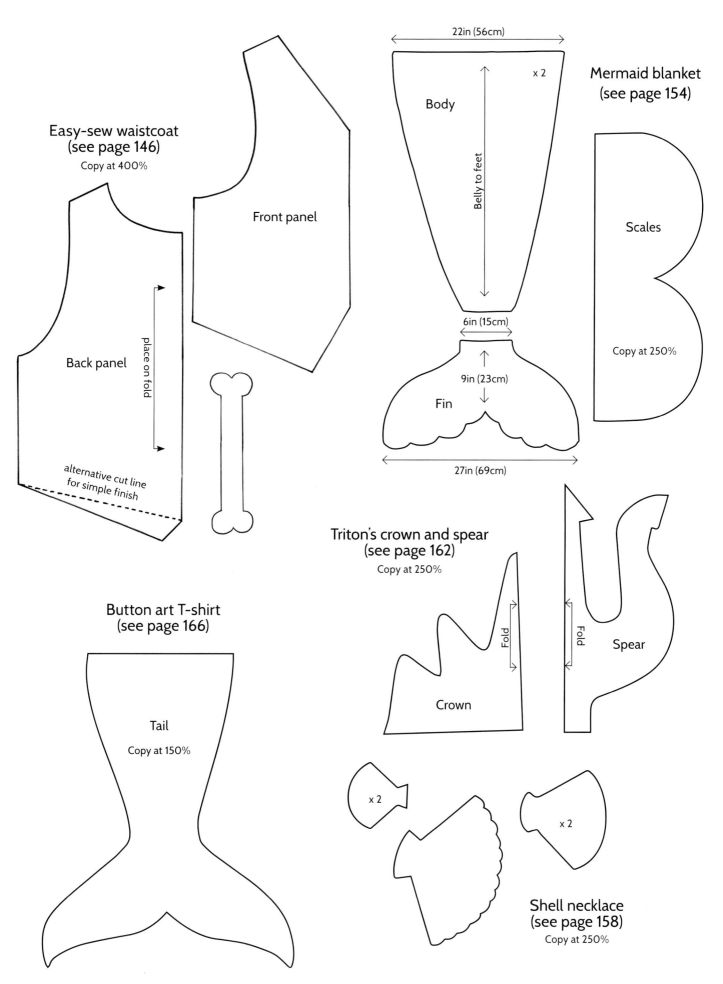

Easy-sew waistcoat
(see page 146)
Copy at 400%

Front panel

Back panel

place on fold

alternative cut line
for simple finish

Mermaid blanket
(see page 154)

x 2

Body

Belly to feet

22in (56cm)

Scales

Copy at 250%

6in (15cm)

9in (23cm)

Fin

27in (69cm)

Button art T-shirt
(see page 166)

Tail

Copy at 150%

Triton's crown and spear
(see page 162)
Copy at 250%

Fold

Fold

Spear

Crown

x 2

x 2

Shell necklace
(see page 158)
Copy at 250%

175

First published 2019 by
Guild of Master Craftsman Publications Ltd,
Castle Place, 166 High Street, Lewes, East Sussex BN7 1XU, UK

ISBN 978 1 78494 517 6

While every effort has been made to obtain permission from the copyright holders for all material used in this book, the publishers will be pleased to hear from anyone who has not been appropriately acknowledged and to make the correction in future reprints.

The publishers and authors can accept no legal responsibility for any consequences arising from the application of information, advice or instructions given in this publication.

A catalog record for this book is available from the British Library.

Publisher: Jonathan Bailey
Production: Jim Bulley and Jo Pallett
Senior Project Editor: Wendy McAngus
Managing Art Editor: Gilda Pacitti
Designer: Luana Gobbo
Photographers: Chris Gloag, Andrew Perris and Emma Sekhon
Step-by-step photography: Laura Minter and Tia Williams
Additional photographs and cover illustrations: Shutterstock.com

Colour origination by GMC Reprographics
Printed and bound in China

To order a book, or to request a catalog, contact:

GMC Publications Ltd
Castle Place, 166 High Street, Lewes,
East Sussex BN7 1XU, United Kingdom

Tel: +44 (0)1273 488005
www.gmcbooks.com